# WICKED PLEASURES

## Meditations on the Seven "Deadly" Sins

Edited by
ROBERT C. SOLOMON

ROWMAN & LITTLEFIELD PUBLISHERS, INC.
*Lanham • Boulder • New York • Oxford*

ROWMAN & LITTLEFIELD PUBLISHERS, INC.

Published in the United States of America
by Rowman & Littlefield Publishers, Inc.
4720 Boston Way, Lanham, Maryland 20706
www.rowmanlittlefield.com

12 Hid's Copse Road
Cumnor Hill, Oxford OX2 9JJ, England

Copyright © 1999 by Robert C. Solomon
First paperback printing 2001

British Library Cataloguing in Publication Information Available

The hardback edition of this book was previously cataloged by the Library of Congress as
follows:

Solomon, Robert C.
    Wicked pleasures : meditations on the seven "deadly" sins / edited by
Robert C. Solomon.
        p. cm.
    Includes bibliographical references and index.
    ISBN 0-8476-9250-7 (hardcover : alk. paper)
    1. Deadly sins. I.Title.
    BV4626.S65        1999
    241'.3—dc21                                                        98-27047
                                                                       CIP

ISBN 0-8476-9250-7 (cloth : alk. paper)
ISBN 0-7425-0845-5 (pbk. : alk. paper)

Printed in the United States of America

♾™ The paper used in this publication meets the minimum requirements of American
National Standard for Information Sciences—Permanence of Paper for Printed Library
Materials, ANSI/NISO Z39.48–1992.

# CONTENTS

# PREFACE

The seven deadly sins have provided gossip, amusement, morality plays, and plots for nearly fifteen hundred years. The sins themselves have always been popular and pervasive, of course, but the number seven and that dubious "deadly" have long invited speculation as well. The classic heptalog was instituted by Pope Gregory the First, also known as "the Great," who in a more charming mood was responsible for the liturgical chanting still associated with his name. His list of seven was confirmed and reasserted by Saint Thomas Aquinas, and it has been reproduced, whether in sermons or in games of Trivial Pursuit, ever since. The list survived the Reformation, the Inquisition, the Enlightenment, pop-tent evangelism, secular humanism, quantum theory, postmodernism, the Nixon and Clinton administrations, the writings of innumerable rabbis and Christian moralists, two series in the *New York Times*, and many bad movies, the most recent entitled, unimaginatively, *Seven*. I have no doubt that the list—not to mention the sins themselves—will survive these somewhat skeptical meditations and reflections as well.

The idea for this book was suggested to me by Jennifer Ruark and was helped along by Jonathan Sisk, Christa Acampora, and Maureen MacGrogan, all of Rowman & Littlefield. The seven contributors were cooperative from the first and responsive to my suggestions; they have made the book what it is. Special thanks to Melanie Jackson, my agent, both for setting up the project and for her help in obtaining the rights to Thomas Pynchon's piece. I thank my many friends past and present who have schooled me and shared with me every one of the naughty seven, and I offer loving thanks to Kathy Higgins for guiding me through a new life relatively devoid of sins. Thanks also to Jenene Allison, who has also taught me a few new things about them.

# INTRODUCTION

A round the north portal of the great cathedral in Strasbourg, France, ten contorted, grimacing trolls, representing the vices, lie crushed under the weight (and the weapons) of an equal number of life-size, standing, quite lovely young women, presumably virgins, representing the virtues. Such is the traditional iconography of vice and virtue, the latter trampling the former. The vices are represented as diminutive and pathetic, barely human, while the virtues are almost invariably portrayed in terms of unblemished (and untouchable) human perfection. Our vices render us less than fully human, while our virtues goad us to be more than human, even saintly.

The vices have always had a bad rap, especially when they get reclassified as "sins," that is, as offenses not only against taste and social propriety but against God himself. But then again, isn't it obvious that these so-called sins are in fact the very stuff of life, the hot, puffy, humiliating, pathetic, but essential ingredients in that human comedy that began with the expulsion from the Garden of Eden? The virtues, by contrast, all too often tend to be humorless, self-righteous, cool, even cold, like their statuesque counterparts on Strasbourg's north portal. Even such virtues as congeniality, wit, and charm sometimes betray the chilly smoothness of habits too polished, too practiced, too impersonal to be fully convincing. The most convivial virtues, we might dare suggest, may be the most civilized vices, hardly sins, much less "deadly."

## I. THE HUMAN CIRCUS

"The seven deadly sins." Seven is an odd and arbitrary number—despite a long numerological and mystical literature celebrating the supposed

1

magic of seven, and this particular seven is an unusual collection of human foibles. *Sloth, greed, gluttony, anger, lust, envy,* and *pride.* None of them is particularly hateful or vicious. They are far more the stuff of gossip and sitcoms than the target of moral philosophy. They are a very mixed bunch: the first of them mentioned, sloth, is marked by a deficiency of ambition; the last, pride, by an exaggeration of self-worth. Anger suggests loss of control but more importantly self-righteous indignation and dangerous vengefulness. Envy embellishes invidious comparison with frustration of desire. The other four might be characterized as straightforward excesses of desire. They are all intimately familiar to us. They are not rare violations or breakdowns of civility, much less the undoing of a perverse species, but rather routine and mundane features of human behavior. "Human-all-too-human," Friedrich Nietzsche would say.

Nietzsche found vices galore in the human circus, many of them truly fatal, but the "deadly" seven were not among them. Indeed, real human viciousness and brutality—cruelty, savagery, indifference to human suffering, tyranny, ethnic hatred, religious persecution, and racial bigotry—don't even make the list. Nor do lying, cheating, stealing, adultery, drunkenness, or murder. (Why is drinking—and intoxication in general—not among the seven? Perhaps it is not irrelevant that old Aquinas loved a nip, not to mention the Lord himself at that fateful, final supper. Noah's drunkenness replenished the species, after all, and the best beers, wines, and brandies have long provided the main source of income for monasteries in Europe.) To be sure, murder violates one of the most holy commandments of the Judeo-Christian tradition. But yet, to just state the obvious, its absence on the list of the "deadly" is conspicuous.

Among the many man-made evils in the world, the "deadly" seven barely jiggle the scales of justice, and it is hard to imagine why God would bother to raise a celestial eyebrow about them; in other words, why they would rate as sins at all. A clever theologian might argue that the sin is an offense against God's cosmic order rather than an offense against God, personally, but our raised-eyebrow query remains the same: why would such trivial and ordinary behavior disturb either God's order or God? Leave aside the big question—why did He create sinners, knowing that they were going to sin (even assuming that sins are acts of "free will")—and we are still left with the odd portrait of a God of infinite concerns and capacities being bothered by a bloke who can't get out of bed, or takes one too many peeks at a naughty *Playboy* pictorial, or scarfs down three extra jelly doughnuts, or has a nasty thought about his neighbor. And yet the very meaning of "deadly"—linguistic slippage, possibly, from the less lethal word "mortal"—refers to the loss of one's soul, condemnation to hell. Other sins, a small lie for instance, may simply be "venial," a step on the path but not a slip on the slope to damnation. The deadly seven sins, however human or humorous they may appear, are therefore not funny, nor foibles, nor mere human flaws, but among the very worst of our numerous human burdens.

If the seven sins are "deadly" in any sense, perhaps, it is because of their apparent innocuousness, their insidious subversiveness, their undeniable ordinariness. They may have their origins in minor lapses, untempered impulses, unchecked childhood habits. They thus slip in, like a parasite that may lie in wait for years and does its damage slowly, cumulatively, until somewhere around middle age—what we rather dubiously call "maturity." Then sin appears, as if born full-blown, betraying the unsightly symptoms of a lifetime gone somewhat to seed. It is sin that gives us each "the face that we deserve"—the grimace of envy, the scowl of anger, the leer of lust, the puffy arrogance of pride, the droopiness of sloth, the hungry eyes and slight drool of greed and gluttony.

The so-called sins are more embarrassing than deadly, more self-frustrating than lethal. But they may seem to be deadly insofar as, once established, they are all but impossible to get rid of. Libido may diminish with age but lust continues, even more unseemly as lechery. Or the sin may metamorphose into envy or anger, two emotions whose habit it is to feed on themselves, growing more obsessive even as they prove to be less effective. Lust can be sublimated into gluttony, where satisfaction is easier to come by, and, of course, it can be transformed into greed, where "more" has no logical terminus. "Better than sex," boasts a Wall Street trader in the midst of a boom, "and no end in sight!"

## II. SEVEN?

Why *seven?* Why not ten, or perhaps only one or two? This, too, is instructive. Seven is an ancient magical number that retained tremendous symbolic significance throughout the Middle Ages. One gets the impression that identity of the specific sins is almost arbitrary, so long as that sacred quota is fulfilled. Before Gregory there was a list of eight, and there has always been some interplay with the Ten Commandments. Throughout history, there have been any number of attempts to reduce all of the sins to one—pride, for example, or gluttony. There have been ferocious debates on the matter. But the magic of the number seven has dominated. It is the perfect number, according to Pythagoras (the sum of three plus four, both lucky too). There are seven hills of Rome, and seven was thought to be the number of the planets. There are seven notes on the Lyre of Hermes (and thus seven notes in the Pythagorean musical scale), and, of course, seven days of the week, seven days of creation (counting the Sabbath), seven bodies in alchemy, seven trumpets at Jericho, seven altars of Balsam, seven-week feasts, the dance of the seven veils, the seventh son of the seventh son, and the seven-year itch. The Muslim had seven heavens, T. E. Lawrence rediscovered seven pillars of wisdom, and Christ had seven last things to say. If God himself were to enumerate sins, he would surely make their number equal to the number of days or, more to the point, make the number of vices equal the number of virtues. Of these, there were seven: the Greek and Roman ("cardinal") virtues of prudence, fortitude, temperance, and justice, combined with the three Christian ("theological") virtues: faith, hope, and charity. One surmises that human psychology played a relatively small role in this enumeration. No matter how varied our foibles, numerology was definitive. *Hebdomania.* The precise number and hierarchy of sins aside, the attempt to catalog and rank the sins bespeaks a certain legalism that has characterized our efforts to come to terms with and contain human frailties, misdemeanors, and crimes.

## III. THE DOCTRINE OF THE MEAN

Understandably, but all too often, the sins are characterized—or caricatured—by their most vulgar and humiliating excesses. Late-medieval artists went out of their way to portray the sins as monstrous and repulsive, hardly human. And, of course, we can always see the great crimes and evils of history as an elaboration of vice, the wrath of Attila or Genghis Khan, the megalomanic pride of a Hitler or a Stalin, the greed of the suburban developer, the real-life Lolita-lust of a non-Nabokovian

Humbert. But, even short of crime and evil, the vices are rarely given their due. Gluttony, for example, is not usually depicted in terms of an elegant but outrageously opulent Michelin three-star Menu du Soir dinner. (The French term *gourmand* has much to recommend it in this regard.) Gluttony is rather depicted in porcine fashion. The glutton is almost invariably fat and badly dressed, shirttails draping a bulging belly, and his (more rarely her) table manners not even fit for a pig (sauces dripping down multiple chins, fistfuls of food traffic-jammed into the hippopotamus-sized mouth, interrupted only by the occasional gasp for breath or pungent eruption of gas).

So, too, lust is almost always depicted as wild-eyed and drooling, hopelessly priapic (in the male incarnation), vaginally voracious and insatiable (in the female version). The lovely lust that so often accompanies love—in its Aristophanic sense, of course—sweet and sensitive, as well as exquisitely insatiable, is quite conscientiously omitted from this obscene eroticism. ("If it's love, it's not lust, if it's lust, it's not love" goes the simpleminded argument.) Sloth, according to the same excessive stereotypes, cannot even get out of bed. So, too, anger is depicted red-faced, out of control, hateful, unreasonable. But righteous anger, not anger that is self-righteous but anger that is right, warranted, justified—outrage at an egregious injustice, for example—doesn't fit the stereotype of the explosive petty tyrant who uses his or her anger to intimidate or manipulate or merely to express hostility.

But excesses do not define the vices. They are, we might say, only the potential vices of the vices. And vices are not only excesses (or excesses of excesses); they are also deficiencies. Thus Aristotle defended a doctrine that is usually called "the doctrine of the mean." The idea, which he intended as something of a definition or criterion of virtue, centered on the notion that the virtues were neither deficiencies nor excesses (courage as neither recklessness nor cowardice, for example). That would mean that seven virtues (although Aristotle had no neat list) would imply *fourteen* vices. But this would be numerologically unacceptable, and so the standard view remains the less insightful one—that the virtues and vices are opposites, one vice for every virtue.

David Hume, for instance, suggests such a polarity by reducing virtues to qualities "pleasing and useful to ourselves and others" and vice, accordingly, as not so. As his prime examples, Hume considers pride, one of the supposed seven sins, which he defends as a virtue, as opposed to humility, which he calls (ironically) "a monkish virtue"—in other words, a vice. Hume is brilliant and cunning in his conceptual somersaults (most famously, his twisting around of reason's dominance over the passions: "reason is and ought to be the slave of the passions"), but in this instance, we have to insist that vice is not simply lack of virtue (nor is virtue simply lack of vice). There are parallels and oppositions to be discovered (or invented) between sloth, greed, gluttony, anger, lust, envy, and pride, on the one hand, and prudence, fortitude, temperance, justice, faith, hope, and charity, on the other, to be sure. But the two lists of seven and seven display an appalling lack of symmetry and the supposed oppositions an obvious lack of rigor. Human virtue and vice do not form a binary system but rather an organic complex of interlocking habits, emotions, conceptions, compulsions, and sensitivities. The virtues that make someone admirable may be the very same vices that make them annoying, and the vices that make someone interesting thus become their virtues.

Could one possibly defend a "doctrine of the mean" regarding the seven sins, or vices? Lust in excess, inappropriate sexual craving, eroticism that forgets its manners may be repulsive, but isn't there also something pathetic about the absence or loss of libido, about frigidity and impotence? A healthy lust, on the other hand, may be nothing less than love, even a "lust for life." So, too, scarfing down a greasy meal fit for a slob may be disgusting, but a self-righteous dieter or health-food fanatic without appetite or taste, who looks down disapprovingly at the delicacies enjoyed by others, is also a poor choice for a dinner companion. Two cheers, at least, for the appetites, which allow our potential for enjoyment to ever renew itself. Why must philosophers degrade them as vices, much less count them as sins? Triangulated among sloth, envy, and greed lies healthy ambition, the mean in the midst of three extremes. The absence of pride may not be modesty or humility but something loathsome and self-destructive, and the inability to get angry makes one not a saint but, as Aristotle pointedly insisted, a "dolt." The absence of vice may itself be vice, and nonexcessive and appropriate vice may be nothing less than virtue.

Aristotle also defended a doctrine called "the unity of the virtues." That idea, which admits of many rather absurd interpretations, is that the virtues tend to reinforce one another. Thus, if one has one virtue, one is more likely to have others, and the virtuous person most likely has them all. But so too with the vices, as moralists have often pointed out. Whether or not the precise enumeration of the deadly sins is arbitrary, it must be admitted they often make good company for one another. Greed, lust, and gluttony provide easy if not admirable mutual companionship. Anger and envy often walk hand in hand, sometimes accompanied by pride and sloth, who otherwise tend to be loners. But, then again, Nietzsche countered Aristotle with the equally plausible thesis that we might call "the dis-unity of the virtues," easily extended to the vices as well. Each virtue or vice, Nietzsche says, has a desire for dominance, its own "will to power." Honesty, like lust, tends to shoulder aside competing demands from other virtues and vices. And even more tempting: sometimes virtue forms an effective partnership with vice such that their unity tends to obscure the distinction altogether. When anger, envy, and justice join forces, watch out!

## IV. IT'S THE THOUGHT THAT COUNTS

Saint Thomas Aquinas was onto something big when—original sin notwithstanding—he insisted that every sin must be a *doing,* not an affliction or a mere personal flaw. To be sure, the doing in question might be little more than a thought, but thoughts can be entertained and encouraged. Thoughts can be provoked into intentions and prodded into expressions, gestures, words, and actions. There is the expressive punch that is provoked by anger, or at least the clenched fist and the red-faced glare. There is the clandestine visit to the nearest motel room that consummates lust, the self-serving but ill-considered boast that proclaims one's pride, the Faustian land deal that manifests greed. Where there are no such consequences or manifestations, at the very least a facial expression or a gesture, we are rightly hesitant to talk of vice at all, although God, being everywhere and all-knowing, may spy sin nevertheless.

The notion of sin, though not of vice, is that it is an offense in the eyes of God, who sees everything, and not just in the eyes of men and women, who do not. Thus the shift from pagan vices to Christian sins involves a serious change in the moral rules. Vices are vices only to the extent that they have public manifestations, however subtle and self-contained. The nature of sin, by contrast, is that it is the thought that counts. Of course intention and action aggravate the charge: a leering look is worse than a lustful fantasy and an inappropriate caress or fondle much worse then either. Yet, to think lustful thoughts, as Jimmy Carter confessed prior to the 1976 presidential election, is to already "have lust in one's heart." Sin is of the soul, and only secondarily a matter of expression and behavior. A thought, Old Thomas tells us, is an act; so the thought leads us to motive, which can yield to intention, which is productive of action. It is all a function of the will, and thus blameworthy. Nevertheless, we readily ignore such confessions as Carter's—we even view them as quaint. We rather focus on full-blooded actions. We want our sins to be robust, not mere thoughts. Thus, understandably, without God's X-ray vision, we focus on manifestations and consequences, what gets witnessed not only by God but by the paparazzi and captured in the tabloids. And the wages of sin, we have come to learn, can add up to seven figures.

The virtues and vices are often said to be good or bad (respectively) "in themselves," not in terms of their consequences or their potential embarrassments. It is simply *wrong* to feel lust, to be greedy, to envy, to nourish undeserved pride. What theological doctrine adds to the insight that sin is thought is God the omnipresent if beneficent judge. Nevertheless, none of the seven sins seems sufficiently serious to attract God's attention, no matter that He has infinite capacity for detail. (Nietzsche declares "God is dead," in part to capture the tedium and banality of such a conception.) Of course the various sins and vices attract *our* attention, if only because we share them, or at least recognize in ourselves their potential. How much of our gossip about others' vices is a strategy of taking the offensive, to hide and protect, to justify or excuse, our own? How much of our gossip is a matter of compensation, of rationalization, of *ressentiment*? How much of our condemnation of lust and greed, for instance, is envy? How much of our condemnation of sloth is a tacit defense of greed, and vice versa? ("Why would anyone want to work so hard? How can they even find time to spend the money?") One might say that other people's sins are so important to us only because of our own sins, and what motivates our interest, as H. L. Mencken famously observed, is "the worry that someone, somewhere, might be having a good time." That is the thought that counts.

## V. ETHICS FOR LOSERS

Against the deadly seven, but without going back to real evil, let's juxtapose a real vice. Gambling—that is a vice. (Why not a sin as well? Because gamblers refuse to see the world as merely a product of chance, and frequently appeal to divine guidance if not also divine intervention on their route to secular hell?) As a gambler, you can lose all your money, lose your home, but first and foremost you lose your reason, your pride, your common sense, and eventually your humanity. You deprive and then cheat and probably steal from your family, your friends, your employer. Despite the odds—which always seem to be in your favor—you deny the obvious. You become self-deceptive, pathologically compulsive, convinced that, eventually, you must win. Gambling destroys your life, and not just your life alone. It contorts your mind, demolishes your values, makes you a pariah to all but your fellow addicts. That is the nature of vice, real vice. And compared to that, what is sloth other than a sometimes infuriating lack of get-up-and-go?

To be sure, sloth may be a career liability in this hustle-and-bustle age, but the couch potato is less often the object of scorn than the target of hopeful advertisers. There are gadgets to implement rather than correct the so-called vice (remote control television, in particular, comes to mind). Especially in these overscheduled times, sloth more often manifests as "laid-back," a virtue rather than a vice. But even as a career impediment, it hardly counts as a sin, an offense against God. Of course, Saint Thomas thought of sloth as laxness of faith, but there is very little reason to think that the seven deadly sins have maintained their offensiveness in God's eyes, or for that matter in the often harsh opinions of the church, or rather churches, which now often encourage the vices rather than preach against them.

The truth is that the mortal sins have been reduced—and perhaps have always been—to just the most noticeable if on occasion annoying as well as amusing aspects of human nature, our character as a species. Sloth has become an aspiration. (On bumper stickers across the nation we read, "I'd rather be fishin'.") So, too, greed became the all-American emotion (back in the eighties) before it was replaced by nineties rage (not mere anger) in the national temperament. Lust is sold as an elixir to the middle class (though it has always been a profitable commodity among the better-off leisure classes), and excessive, uncritical, often pointless pride is marketed even in the schools (at least in California) as "self-esteem."

Then there is squinty, green-eyed envy. On the one hand, envy too is essential to the consumer economy and, consequently, to our somewhat confused conception of the social. Helmut Schoeck, in a perverse tome several decades ago, defended envy as the key to a healthy society. In advertising, "keeping up with the Joneses" represents the consumerist creed. It is motivated, undeniably, by envy. (In the new global economy, the scope of envy is enormously expanded, but the cross-cultural motive remains the same: "if they have it, we want it too.") But, on the other hand, compare envy to resentment, a much more vicious and vindictive emotion, and therefore much more dangerous. Or compare it to spite, which is by its very nature more violent and self-destructive. The truth is that envy, in the register of "negative" emotions, is only pathetic. It is a loser's emotion. It is hardly a vice, or a sin. True, in Shakespeare's Iago it can lead to great mischief and even murder, but the pathetic truth about envy is that it isn't usually even clever or capable. Indeed, that's why it's envy, because it is an impotent longing, without rights or entitlement, without power, without a clue. According to Catholic tradition, envy leads first to sadness, then to gossip, then to *Schadenfreude,* then to hatred (*New Catholic Encyclopedia,* p. 642). But often, envy tends to simmer in its own juices, a danger to no one but oneself. It is the one sin, contra Schoeck, not worth having at all.

## VI.  HEAVEN AS HEALTH CLUB

Why, in our sunny, secular, selfish, often vulgar, "greed is good" society, would the sins still be taken seriously? Here is a hypothesis, fit for the day. What are (archaically) called the "deadly sins" have nothing to do with damnation or degeneracy but rather with *poor health.* They lead to a reduced lifespan, an unappealing appearance, the inability to attract a mate at the health club. What is deadly about the deadly sins is that, literally, they shorten our lives. Thus gluttony is really a code name for calories and high cholesterol. Lust is short for overdoing it, endangering one's health, wasting one's "precious bodily fluids" *(Dr. Strangelove).* For the less adventurous or simply unsuccessful, there is excessive masturbation, long high on the list of physiological dangers to both body and soul. Sloth now means not getting enough exercise. Greed is taking on more than you can handle, inducing dangerous stress. Pride becomes an excuse not to exercise, and envy is just another excuse not to try. Of course, health isn't everything, but that seems to be a fact that surpasses current popular understanding. In any case, it seems to be an easy, contemporary, and totally secular way of appreciating what Aquinas and all those other church fathers were going on about. The seven deadlies are not sins (except in the sense that triple-fudge chocolate cake is a sin), not vices (except in the sense that smoking is a vice), not offenses against God but against yourself—not your soul but your body and thus, perhaps, an offense against your doctor. But with our new managed health care plans, we can rest assured that he or she, too, no longer cares.

But health worries are often disguises for spiritual concerns. What is promulgated as good for the body is often a denial of the body, an attack on the body; and the attack on the seven sins is, more to the metaphysical point, an attack on the human body. It is the body itself that is sinful, as Adam and Eve revealed with those miserable fig leaves. Not the genitals but biology as such is the source of our embarrassment, our sinfulness before God. Indeed, what is surprising, from this point of view, is how few sins there are. Why not salivating, certainly spitting, farting, belching, bad breath, uncontrolled dandruff, and sweating—all of which are proscribed by the media and cured by readily available pharmaceuticals where mere self-control does not suffice? And then there is eating in general and swallowing in particular, not to mention that which follows. Of course, you say, eating is necessary to keep us alive, but what is really necessary is nutrition, not eating. What limited, unspiritual, impious imaginations we have, to think that nutrition requires an activity so disgusting, so fraught with secretions and the excitation of the senses, which is so easily pleasurable, which requires so much preparation and planning, which has as its side effects mucous and feces and bad smells. Surely these could be minimized. Surely the body could be minimized. The ultimate sin, on this account, is gluttony, and gluttony, if unavoidable, means any eating at all. (Anorexia is thus a virtue, as it has often been perceived to be, but bulimia, we should note, is doubly a vice.) All vice could thus be viewed as extensions of breastfeeding, the original sin, followed in due course by snacking, feasting, and dining. It has often been noted (though there is room for much personal disagreement here) that the excesses of the dinner table prompt the excesses of love, as they do sloth. A full belly gives a man pride—has any American president surpassed the proud demeanor of William Howard Taft?—while a more delicious-looking entrée on the plate of one's dinner companion evokes envy. Greed first appears at the nipple, pigs out over Big Macs and generous bowls of mashed potatoes, and ends up playing the commodities futures markets, with relish.

## VII. ON HUMAN NATURE

A different tradition notion, leaving aside the theology of sinfulness, is that the seven deadly sins—or, better, seven daily vices—are simply ordinary human *weaknesses*. That is to say, they are nothing more (nor less) than human nature, human frailty, human finitude. This would distinguish them from the more vicious vices, whose intentions are more blameworthy, whose consequences are more severe, whose victims are more badly battered. It would also throw into question Aquinas's insistence that the sins are voluntary, of the will, rather than afflictions. But the adjective "human" is important, and suggests why the will cannot be completely excluded. Dogs are certainly gluttons (in fact, they make pigs of themselves), but we do not (usually) think it sensible to chastize a dog for gluttony. Dogs want but, in the Thomist sense, they do not will. Rabbits and other rodents are primed to reproduce, but we do not bother to call them "lustful" or "lascivious." The great apes, our nearest and most endangered kin, display many human excesses, particularly those that have to do with politics, but the language of sin and vice seems inappropriate to them. It is *human* weakness that concerns us, human because we are human, human because we will, human because we expect something more of ourselves, human because we think we are more than mere nature. "Nature," insists a very virtuous Kate Hepburn to a vice-ridden Humphrey Bogart on the *African Queen*, "is what we are put on this earth to rise above."

The very possibility of vice and virtue lies in this belief that we are better than the animals, closer to God or, at least, more akin to the angels. We can rise above nature. But isn't this itself the sin of pride, what the Greeks used to call hubris? Perhaps we should interrupt our gossiping and, instead of looking so disparagingly at vice, look at our conceptions of ourselves, our expectations of ourselves, our arrogant insistence on being better than or above nature, our belief that we are essentially spiritual beings, not in the unassailable sense that we have spiritual needs but in the dubious metaphysical sense that we can distinguish our selves from our bodies, master the latter, and deny it its due.

For what we call human weakness may just be being human, and virtue and vice represent not the spirit versus the flesh but spirited flesh looking out for itself, sometimes wisely, sometimes foolishly, sometimes selfishly, but always as flesh.

This is not to defend vice, of course, nor to say that we cannot strive for ideals that challenge or sublimate our natural drives. We can and we do choose to view vice as a challenge, sin as a test (like that original apple in the Garden), and it is one of our undeniable virtues that we do interrogate and cross-examine Mother Nature. But is it so clear that the vices are natural, the product of nature and not society? It is nature that dictates the desire for sex and the need for food, but this is not yet lust and gluttony. In any society that makes sex a scarce but precious commodity, lust will always outstrip any natural desire, and where food (not to mention fat) takes on all sorts of symbolic forms, gluttony is hardly "natural." It is the nature of human society that dictates the vices, not only what is to *count* as vice but the motivation of the vices themselves.

Jean-Jacques Rousseau attributed the majority of the seven sins to the artifices and "corruptions" of society. He was even willing to argue that human nature was basically good, which is to say, without vice. It is through the artifices of society that we learn not only the possibilities but the need for vice. Where would lust be if—as the Swiss libertine lustily imagined—we mated casually in the woods, on (male) demand, as it were, and went merrily on our way? Where would gluttony, greed, and envy be if there were no private property, if there were only the sweet, lush vegetation of the forests of Saint-Germain? What is pride, but almost unnatural concern with one's standing in court, or in college or in the corporate hierarchy? What is anger but our pride thwarted, passed over for promotion or snubbed by the Dean or the Queen? Of course, Jean-Jacques was opposed by most of the great thinkers of the preceding century, Thomas Hobbes and Bernard Mandeville, for instance, who held the more sociable view that all vice was rooted in natural selfishness, and it remained for the great scottish "worldly" philosopher Adam Smith to pull the ultimate rabbit out of the theoretical hat and show that out of selfishness could come prosperity if not virtue. But that, of course, is another story, though one that would quickly lead us back to greed. According to some of our recent business pundits, fictionally but accurately represented by Oliver Stone's Gordon Gekko, greed has become the most natural as well as beneficial of sins, encompassing (except, perhaps, for sloth) all of the rest. But is there any question here that Wall Street is not an expression of nature?

## VIII. ON MODERATION

The claim that vice is a weakness has its obvious attractions. It reintroduces the victim mentality, allowing if not encouraging the excuses and rationalizations that are themselves among our most human vices. "I can't help it" is the routine complaint of the sinner, and the possibility of grace and absolution only reinforces this conceit. But the idea that vice is a weakness also suggests that avoiding vice, overcoming vice, requires strength. This may be illusory, even self-congratulatory, as Nietzsche, a man of few vices, pointed out a century ago. Against "the moralists' mania which demands not the control but the extirpation of the passions," he argued, "their conclusion is ever: only the emasculated man is the good man" (*Antichrist,* 47). A man without lust may just be impotent, and a man who will not get angry, who "turns the other cheek," may just be a coward or, as Aristotle insisted, a fool. A modest eater may just not like food (as Franz Kafka ironically argues in his story "The Hunger Artist"), and a person without pride may simply recognize that he or she has nothing to be proud of.

The idea of virtue as victorious over vice looms large in those medieval cathedrals and accounts of the virtues, but the modern pretense that virtue requires strength may be just the same self-deception or, worse, self-rightousness based on the false supposition that *not doing* is more difficult than *doing* (the case of sloth obviously excepted). There is much to be said in favor of "discipline," but mediocrity, banality, and impotence should not be confused with the discipline of self-control. This is what Nietzsche called "slave morality," turning the tables on those who enjoy themselves by declaring their pleasures sinful (even "Evil") and holding slavish abstemious selves up for praise as the very model of the Good. Never mind that they themselves secretly lust for those same pleasures but know full well that they are in no position to compete for them. If vice is said to be weakness, then let us not confuse weakness for virtue.

Insofar as vices are matters of *excess,* the best way to overcome them would seem to be "moderation." Of course, Oscar Wilde turned the tables on Aristotle when he variously declared that nothing succeeds like excess and that the only way to get over a temptation is to give in to it. What Wilde was objecting to, however, was not so much moderation as the sleazy moralist's trick of not-so-subtly speeding up the argument such that one races from excess past moderation to abstinence. Thus, lust is bad, because it is an excess of sexual desire, but then, we too quickly conclude, sexual desire must be bad as well. Thus Paul contrives his hateful lesson on marriage ("better than to burn"), and Augustine assures us that Adam, before his exile, managed to "get it up" by sheer will, like a modern porn star, without any desire or libido whatsoever. Gluttony is bad, because it is an excess of appetite, but, we now see, appetite itself is bestial, lowly, humiliating, and best satisfied by as little as possible. Pride, once a virtue, is a vice because it bespeaks an excess of ego and lack of humility, but then ego itself is put under suspicion, and modesty becomes self-negation, a curious if cloying charm. Thus, again, Nietzsche's suspicion that "the emasculated man is the good man." Indeed, the pervasive problem with talking about sin and vice is that it opens the door to the petty moralist and gives him a foothold in his easy climb to the holy balcony above us, from whence he declares even our moderation to be vicious, if only by virtue of that infamous "slippery slope" down which even the righteous slide unwittingly from innocence into vice.

## IX. LETTING GO

"Control yourself." How much of the language of sin and vice reflects the need to control, the need to take control, a kind of hysteria, "the control-freak"? But where is the willingness to take a chance, to let ourselves go? Indeed, the very phrase "to let oneself go" is an accusation of vice, a suggestion of sloth and the implication of gluttony, greed, and however many other unnamed sins of omission and excess. Even our risks are tightly controlled, but "letting ourselves go" is also the way to creativity, adventure, and self-discovery. "Letting go" can also be a religious conception, not only for the ebullient Charismatics but implicit in the very language of submission (*islām,* Arabic). What is our sense of ourselves such that we need such self-control? What conception of the "it" inside of us, or of our very selves, inspires such terror? Why do we feel the need to so starkly contrast will with weakness, control with chaos? Why do we feel the need to so starkly contrast vice with virtue, and sin with grace?

Nietzsche praised self-discipline, self-mastery, but he talked even more about the "love of fate," the "Dionysian" ideal of total abandonment. The link between the two he saw as *style,* the cultivation of one's character, beyond the false distinction between virtue and vice ("Good and Evil"). "Give style to your character," Nietzsche urges, in his *Gay Science.* Control need not be virtue, and self-abandonment need be no vice. It all depends, one might say, on what it is that is being controlled and who it is that is doing the abandoning. The worst sin, perhaps, is neglecting or denying one's own talents, and that bit of wisdom comes not from Nietzsche but from the very virtuous Immanuel Kant.

"Letting go." Can we really deny the joy, even the envy, we feel, looking at someone who just doesn't care? I am thinking of two sex divinities of the past, Anita Ekberg (of *La Dolce Vita*) and Marlon Brando (of *Streetcar,* not *The Godfather*), both of whom "let themselves go" to voluminous excess. Of course, they are the butt of jokes and late-night satire, but they also seem to illustrate some basic truth, some inescapable irony. We gleefully imitate the disgustingly expansive character in Monty Phython's *The Meaning of Life* as we ourselves request, only half-jokingly, *"the lot!"* "Letting ourselves go" is a delightful fantasy, however disgusting it may be. It has very much to do with being human, which is not a weakness but, from a truly humanistic perspective, a thing of beauty. Where there is love, what does it mean to speak of vice? Where there is beauty, why talk of sin?

## X. TO SIN

The seven essays that follow examine the convolutions and subtleties of the arbitrarily but now traditionally designated seven deadly sins. The essays do not reflect the vices of their authors, nor does the choice of authors and their vices reflect the good opinion of the editor of any of them. Rather, like all good essays, authors, and vices, they are exemplary in their individuality. I provided only minimal guidelines or instructions, and they responded as I hoped they would, with creative, sensitive, sometimes scholarly, always thoughtful, often very funny, and personal pieces. In what follows, William Miller writes on gluttony, Jerry Neu on pride, Thomas Pynchon on sloth, James Ogilvy on greed, Elizabeth Spelman on anger, William Gass on lust, and Don Herzog on envy. Being free of these vices myself, I have left them and their essays to their own, often ingenious devices.

But now, to sin—beginning, as Great Gregory suggested, with the omnivorous sin of gluttony.

# 1

# GLUTTONY

## William Ian Miller

Among them all, who can descry
A vice more mean than Gluttony?
Of any groveling slave of sense,
Not one can claim so small pretense
To that indulgence which the wise
Allow to human frailties
As the inglorious, beastly sinner,
Whose only object is—a dinner.

—William Combe, 1815[1]

Gluttony does not have the grandeur of pride, the often brilliant strategic meanness of envy and avarice, the glory of wrath. It does manage to gain some small allure by its association with lust, its sexy sibling sin of the flesh. Yet there is something irrevocably unseemly about gluttony, vulgar and lowbrow, self-indulgent in a swinish way. Gluttony is not the stuff of tragedy or epic. Imagine Hamlet too fat to take revenge[2] or Homer making his topic the gluttony of Achilles rather than his wrath. With gluttony, compare pride and anger, sins that mark the grand action of revenge, sins that can be emblematized by tigers, lions, eagles, and hawks, rather than by pigs and (dare I say it) humans. Gluttony requires some immersion in the dank and sour realm of disgust. Gluttony inevitably leads to regurgitation, excrement, hangover, and gas and to despair and feelings of disgust. But it has a cheerier side too that I don't mean to ignore: the delights and pleasures of good food, drink, and convivial joys. If gluttony often drags disgust in its wake, it also

19

motivates a certain kind of amiability that makes for good companionship, hospitality, and even a kind of easygoing benevolence.

Most of the seven deadly sins are less properly sins than dispositions,
tendencies, or traits of character. Nor are they a complete list of sin-
generating dispositions. Fearfulness, for example, is surely a much graver
motivator of sin than gluttony and even pride. Just what is it about
gluttony that makes it a vice? Do the grounds of its viciousness shift
through time? Could one ever claim gluttony a virtue without also being
a shallow hedonist? Even David Hume, who took great delight in making the case for the virtue of pride, was willing to go only half way on
gluttony's behalf, arguing, in effect, that obsessing on its viciousness
meant you were manifesting the unamiable vices of crabbed moralism
and frenzied enthusiasm, not that you were manifesting virtue:

> To imagine, that the gratifying of any sense, or the indulging of any
> delicacy in meat, drink, or apparel is of itself a vice, can never enter
> into a head, that is not disordered by the frenzies of enthusiasm.[3]

We are somewhat conflicted about the precise moral status of gluttony. Indeed, as we shall see, so were earlier ages, although the grounds
of their ambivalence were rather different from ours. Among us the sin
of gluttony is the sin of fat, whether it lolls about men's paunches (note
that fat requires that we rename stomachs "paunches" or "beer-bellies")
or squiggles loosely about women's thighs or clogs the arteries in a gen-
der-neutral fashion. Gluttony for us is the sin of ugliness and ill health,
but chiefly ugliness. Except for philosophers and theologians, most of us
have never managed to distinguish too well between the good and the
beautiful, between the ethical and moral on one hand and the aesthetic
and pleasurable on the other. As a matter of practical morality, ugliness
remains, despite centuries of pious exhortation to the contrary, a sin.
And the very cachet of gluttony's historical pedigree as an honored
member of a select group of capital sins helps relax the grip of any nig-
gling scruples we may have acquired about blaming the fat for their
obesity. There is nothing quite like the sin of fat. Its wages, we are told,
is death—physical, moral, and social. The author of a best-selling how-
to-raise-your-adolescent-daughter book reports that 11 percent of
Americans would abort a fetus if they were told it had a tendency to
obesity. Elementary-school children judge the fat kid in the class more

negatively than they do the bully.[4] In this life, the fat are damned, the beautiful are saved, and we are not sure of anything beyond the grave.

But this is a very recent historical development, for when the poor were thin, fat was beautiful. And when poverty came to be characterized less by insufficient calories and more by too many calories of the wrong kind, fat became ugly. In a perverse way, the poor determine fashion by providing an antimodel of the ideal body type, which the rich then imitate negatively. I will discuss these issues more fully later but let me not loosen my grip on this morsel of an argument without adding the following tidbit: although not all gluttony leads to obesity, nor is all obesity the consequence of the voluntary indulgence in the vice of gluttony, we antigluttonous moralists are never quite willing to pardon fat. The burden of proof, we think, is upon fat people to adduce evidence that they are not gluttons, for fat makes out a prima facie case that they are guilty and thus owe the rest of us an apology or an explanation for having offended.

## A PARTIAL HISTORY OF GLUTTONY

When the first list of the chief sins appeared at the end of the fourth century, there were eight of them and gluttony headed the list.[5] Pride may have been thought more serious, but gluttony still got first billing. Gluttony, doing general service for all the sins of the flesh, was also listed first in the shorter list of the three temptations of Christ, although the temptations never enjoyed the long-running popularity of the seven vices.[6] Gluttony also was listed first by John Cassian who introduced the list of sins to the Latin West in the fifth century, and an occasional writer would see fit to start with gluttony as late as the thirteenth century.[7] Considering that the ordering originated with severe desert ascetics, it was no accident that they listed first what was torturing them most: desires of the flesh, food first, then sex. In the end, however, the ordering of St. Gregory the Great (d. 604) carried the day, and in that order *Superbia* (Pride) claimed its prideful place as first, as made sense for the moral ordering of a less obsessively ascetic and more secularized world; gluttony was stuck back in the pack one step ahead of its sister in the flesh, lust, which figured last.

But the preacher whose topic was gluttony had no problem finding biblical support for claiming its historical preeminence even if it was in some sense less serious a sin than pride and avarice. After all, was it not appetite for the forbidden fruit, desire for that apple that cost us all paradise? Thus Chaucer's Pardoner:

> O glotonye, full of cursednesse!
> O cause first of our confusion!
> O original of our damnation,
> Til Christ had bought us with his blood again!
> Lo, how deare, shortly for to sayn,
> Abought was thilke cursed vileynye!    [thilke = this, such]
> Corrupt was all this world for glotonye.[8]

And considerably earlier in the fourth century St. John Chrysostom was also willing to add the flood to gluttony's rapsheet: "Gluttony turned Adam out of Paradise, gluttony it was that drew down the deluge at the time of Noah."[9] Quite an unsavory beginning for our amiable vice.

To us, Eve has more in common with Prometheus than with the fat lady in the circus. No stretching of Scripture was required to give pride and avarice preeminence. Does not Ecclesiasticus declare pride the beginning of all sin (Sir. 10:13) and St. Paul claim avarice "the root of all evil" (1 Tim. 6:10)? But the image of gluttony as the first sin was persistent. The official homilies of the Anglican church followed the same line. Adam and Eve were gluttonous, said the homilist, and their excesses cost us paradise.[10] Higher-brow theologians, perhaps the highest brow of all, St. Thomas Aquinas, even felt compelled to address the issue of gluttony's priority before dismissing it and asserting the preeminence of pride and avarice.[11]

Whether gluttony is first or penultimate is not so crucial; what is remarkable, however, and this was obsessed upon by medieval and early modern moralists, was just how fertile gluttony was of other vices. The power of a vice to generate other vices was what the theologians understood to make a vice capital. Less rigorous souls—or rigorous souls who doubt their powers to resist a good meal—could argue that gluttony should be winked at: "But is there anyone, O Lord," says a desperate Augustine, "who is never enticed beyond the strict limit of need?"[12] Eating is necessary for life and the blame for lack of measure should be discounted for that reason. But Aquinas concluded that gluttony's productivity of vice was undeniable and the sin was thus unarguably capital.[13]

Gluttony paved the way to lust. It was lust's "forechamber" in the words of a seventeenth-century sermonizer.[14] If in a post-Freudian world we have learned to eroticize food, privileging sex and lust as the prime movers and motivators of virtually all desire, premodern people rather astutely inverted the order. They alimentarized lust. It was food, ingestion, and alimentation in all its forms that provided the dominant metaphors and explanations of motive and desire. No medieval preacher, in his most free-associative moments, ever thought to make lust the first sin or the prime sin. But gluttony sprang immediately to his mind. It was feasts and food that engendered lust. Food and drink come first, as even today they must despite the bad twentieth-century cliché of following sex with the oral gratification of a cigarette. (Should smoking be included within the broad parameters of gluttony? Arguably yes.) In the Wife of Bath's raunchy idiom, "a lickerous (gluttonous) mouth must have a lickerous (lecherous) tail." Notice how the connection between gluttony and lechery was even reproduced at the level of the word *lickerous*. *Lickerous* meant tasty when describing food and gluttonous when describing people or their mouths as in the Wife's quote, but it could also mean lecherous or lascivious as it did when the Wife used it to modify tail. Middle and early modern English supported delightful punning possibilities that followed the Wife in playing suggestively with the homophony of *lickerous, lecherous,* and *lick,* in which genital lust is a handmaid to the larger gluttonous oral order.[15]

In spite of myths perpetuated by pop culture as to the primacy of the genitals, lust still often needs the assist of drink or dietary satiation to dull our initial assessments of the other's desirability or to quell our concerns about the inevitable sacrifice of dignity that comes with indulging lust. Feeding may itself be sufficiently dignity-deflating to pave the way for even greater riskings of it. The picture isn't all as dark as that, for food suggests the delights of conviviality; and conviviality suggests the delights of fleshly pleasure. Most of us find the occasional risks to our dignity well worth it. But can there be any dispute about the relative ordering? At the level of the individual, eating enables fornication which in turn enables the eating of the next generation of fornicators.

Gluttony was also inextricably linked with sloth and this strikes us as perfectly apt. It was only toward the end of the medieval period that sloth started to take on the sense of laziness; medieval sloth was *accidie,* a kind of demoralized despairing torpor of thinking you were excluded from God's grace.[16] It was the nobler medieval version of our contemptible notion: low self-esteem. But sloth had a homelier side too. It was the despair of the morning after, the hangover, the nausea, the heartburn, and headache. William Langland's allegorical Glutton in *Piers Plowman* vomits, passes out drunk, is carried home to bed by his wife where "after all this excess he had an accidie [an attack of sloth]." Langland even alters the traditional ordering of the sins to substitute sloth for lust at gluttony's rear. He gives us a reality check: Lust may indeed follow upon gluttony but that is, in fact, a consummation to be greatly, if not quite devoutly, wished. The grim fact is you mostly end up in bed with a hangover and humiliated, rather than in bed with some delightful enticer of the flesh.

Sloth seems to capture the sense of defeat and shame that are the frequent aftermath of gluttony and lust. It is the shame of having indulged in the present without thought for the future. Or for those binge eaters of today it is the shame of weakness of will, of eating to fill a void that no longer exists in the stomach, but rather in life itself. It is the shame of preferring present sensory satisfaction to present dignity. Sloth is the retreat into primordial ooze. Gluttony thus becomes the fosterer and hence the emblem of all sin that favors instant gratification, the filling of present emptiness with corporeal sensation at the expense of spirit and futurity.

Gluttony was also thought to lead to pride. Food and feasts were the central props in competitive displays, as in a slightly different way people who care about their reputations for discernment in matters of food and wine compete among each other today. In pre-modern and classical times it was not just the quality of food that was at stake in the competition, but glorying in the display and in the expense. Gluttony thus came to be understood as something more than just the swallowing of too much food; it was the whole culture of eating and competitive production for the table that engaged the sin of gluttony.[17] Gluttony and pride, in other words, connived to fuel a form of potlatch. And pride's influence on gluttony justifies the reasonable belief that there may be as much gluttony in the pretentiousness of small and highly produced portions of nouvelle cuisine as in the huge portions and endless replenishments at a Texas barbecue.

Even envy figured in gluttony's retinue. One early fifteenth century gence, like drunk driving is for us. The medieval writer who most directly worried about the distributional aspects of gluttony was Langland. In *Piers Plowman*, every mouthful a glutton took beyond his measurable need was an affront to the poor. Eating was a zero sum game. The more you ate, the less someone else did. And any ingestion beyond what was necessary for the maintenance of life was an act of injustice. Langland's gluttons were the non-producing rich, sturdy beggars who would not work, and above all the friars whose gluttony was undertaken not only in the face of the poor but also in spite of their own vows of poverty. The friars shared with Dives the mantle of personified Gluttony, actually doing him one better by spicing their gluttony with hypocrisy. In Langland's arresting image they "gnaw God in the gorge when their guts are full."[19]

But it is in precisely such an order of scarcity that the impulses to glut are at their greatest. Despair can drive some to live according to the principle of eat, drink, and be merry. Others, more prudent, might be driven to acquire desperately, avariciously in their sense, so as to engorge themselves—not as a form of consumption but as a form of saving. They are literally fatting themselves for the lean times ahead. And this paradoxical method of saving by avidly consuming makes sense when the postponer of gratification would see the grain he had put away ravaged by rats and birds, stolen by humans, rotted by damp, or consumed by fire.

Dives raises another issue that was noted back then. Feasting, though necessarily risking gluttony, was also the occasion for some paltry redistributions from rich to poor, but redistributions nonetheless. Remember that Lazarus received the crumbs from Dives's table. In this regard gluttony can work against avarice. Conviviality means consuming food to be sure, but it also means sharing it and even wasting it so that the human scavengers and gleaners can be nourished. And though Langland spills considerable ink and indignation on wasters who destroy with gluttony what hard workers produce, he is equally indignant when the consuming classes grow less hospitable, curtail the size of their board, and start eating in private so as, he claims, to avoid the claims of the poor for the table scraps:

> Now hath each rich [man] a rule—to eat by himself
> in a private parlor for poor men's sake,

writer, blasting the gluttony of the royal court, recounts that o
consequences of the general gluttony there was the miseries of
lier courtiers who suffered the bitter envy of seeing the best
and best-tasting dishes made available to those higher in the
order, but not to themselves:

> But when these courtiers sit on the benches idle
> Smelling those dishes they bite upon the bridle,
> And then is their pain and anger fell as gall
> When all passeth by and they have naught at all . . .
> Such fish to behold and none thereof to taste,
> Pure envy causeth thy heart near to brast. . . .[18]

Avarice, on the other hand, had an ambivalent and more c
connection with gluttony and one that will take a little more s
work out adequately. We can get at it best by noting that the arc
villainous glutton for the medieval and early modern period was i
as the archetypal avaricious man. He was Dives of the parable of
in Luke 16:19. Dives fared sumptuously every day, and to the m
mind that sumptuous faring was a sign of avarice, or cupidity i
terms, as well as of gluttony. Avarice meant something more th
tightfisted hoarding back then. It meant being overly concerned
acquisition to the exclusion of more spiritual matters. Dives, a
was hardly a miser, but he spent freely on the wrong things and
understood to have been damned eternally for his gluttony and \
This strikes us as a pretty disproportional system of punishment
that Dives's joys were finite—more, in fact, sins of omission, of
blind to the suffering of another, than sins of commission.

But Dives's wrongs were more serious in that earlier moral
than in ours. His avarice and the gluttony are played out in the fa
famished and leprous pauper. And these sins mean something qui
ferent in a world of constant and pressing caloric scarcity. In ai
nomic order in which there is not food enough to go around, in
starvation and famine are always lurking about, gluttony's moral
ratchet up. Gluttony was not just self-indulgence as it mostly is a
inhabitants of developed countries where it imposes on others on
trivial cost of the unpleasantness of seeing the glutton's fat; for that (
economic order, it was, in a sense, murder or a kind of criminal

Or in a chamber with a chimney, and leave the chief hall
that was made for meals, men to eat in,
And all to spare to spill that spend shall another.[20] [spill, spend =
    waste]

The last line scorns avarice of a new sort: the kind that works against
gluttony; the kind that makes for smaller portions, for smaller guest lists,
and for quieter and more civilized company. Civilization, Langland intu-
its long before anyone else does, means not only eating in private but
also saving, deferring consumption, which in turns creates the capital
that will fund the expense of private spaces. It is still too early for Langland to imagine that preventing wastage ("spare to spill") will amount
to any good. He still sees the savings as merely funding another gluttonous waster ("that spend shall another").

    Feasting was also the occasion for conviviality. Chaucer is able with
wit and economy to demonstrate the hospitable amiability of his Franklin simply by giving the generous plenitude of his board a natural energy
of its own: "It snowed in his house of meat and drink."[21] To be too
abstemious about one's food, to put out a spare and meager board, was
to risk giving social offense. Moralists knew this and said that it was a
temptation of the devil to allege reasons of sociability to indulge gluttony. Don't be a party pooper says the fiend: "Dost thou know that
people are calling thee a niggard?"[22] Virtues like sociability, hospitality,
and amiability seemed to require a certain indulgence in gluttony. This
is astute psychology on the part of the devil as well as on the part of the
moralist who understood just how powerful a hold the norms of sociability, generosity, honor, and competitive conviviality have on us. Even
among us, the non-drinker and the vegetarian prompt less praise for
their temperance than wariness and a touch of annoyance for their implicit condemnation of the forms of conviviality. We might be willing
not to behave like pigs, but that does not mean, suggests the devil, that
we have to behave like self-mortifying and joyless desert saints either,
especially when acting in such a matter keeps our purse thick as it thins
our paunch.

    Gluttony in the Middle Ages and early modern period was a sea-
sonal sin. Where there is no refrigeration and storage is more costly than
consumption, more gluttonous consuming goes on when the perishable
foodstuff is ready to eat. So people glutted at harvest and at the late

autumn slaughter of beasts. Orgies of food at certain times were almost a requirement of their state of productivity and technology. Sin it may have been, but they didn't have that much choice. And they would suffer too, to the moralist's mean delight, not only the hangover of the feast but the desperate shortages in early spring when gluttony took the form, not of eating well or fully, but of thinking obsessively about food and where one was to find it. The contrast with our alimentary economy could not be more startling. We can save food, and our production levels are high enough to let us glut day in and day out, spring or fall.

The core of gluttony has always been understood to mean the excessive consumption of food. In the Middle Ages it was assumed that excessive drink was also at the core. In fact, it was via drunkenness that even wrath was admitted to be a mournful consequence of gluttony's powers to generate other sin. The gluttonous drunkard is quick to anger and short on controlling his temper. Genesis's Lot was conventionally cited to show just how bad a fix excessive winebibbery can get you in. In Langland's words:

> Through wine and through women there was Lot encumbered,
> And there begot in gluttony girls [children] that were churls.[23]

But by the late sixteenth century gluttony had come to be seen as more a matter of food than drink, so that one moralist felt it necessary to explain himself when he included drink: "Under Gluttony, I shroud not only excess in meat, but in drink also."[24]

We are psychologically subtle enough to recognize that anorexia and compulsive dieting as well as addiction, bulimia, gourmetism, alcoholism, and any number of irrational and obsessive behaviors regarding the ingestion of food and drink properly belong under the rubric of gluttony. Medieval commentators also understood that gluttony was more than just eating to excess. Following distinctions made by Gregory the Great in the sixth century, writers on vices and virtues well into the fifteenth century understood gluttony to have five main branches: eating too soon, too much, too avidly, too richly in the sense of expensively, and too daintily. One remarkable tradition of medieval writing on the deadly sins subsumed under gluttony all vices of the mouth:[25] lying, backbiting, blaspheming, boasting, perjury, and grumbling, among others. Even heresy and witchcraft, apparently by way of blasphemy, were dealt with under the rubric of gluttony. In this tradition the tavern is seen as the devil's temple in which riotous drinking leads to gambling and swearing and taking God's name in vain.[26]

There is something bizarrely modern about generalizing gluttony to encompass all the sins in which the mouth figures. Freud achieves the same effect by suggesting a matching of each member of the triad of erogenous zones with its particular sin. Gluttony is oral, avarice anal, and lust genital. Each of these vices has its particular pleasure and the prospect of that pleasure is precisely the temptation to indulge it. This contrasts greatly with, say, envy, which is its own punishment, except to the extent it allows for the indirect pleasures of *Schadenfreude*. But food and talk, these are the very substance of oral pleasure and conviviality. The drawbacks come from overindulgence, not from just any indulgence. That is, little gluttonies are pretty much a pleasure pure and simple (the notion of little gluttonies is not incoherent, for even if gluttony by definition means exceeding measure, there is a sense in which excesses can be minor or major); big gluttonies, however, end in the misery of hangover and the heaviness and shame of satiation. The culminating vileness of gluttony is the vileness of vomit and the repeated returning to it in the manner of the dog in Proverbs; the punishment is oral just as the sin is. In this way our physiology seems to be committed to the law of the talion: what by mouth offends shall by mouth make atonement. Both pleasure and pain will focus on the mouth. And in this oral world, spewing foul words is a vomiting forth, revealing one's soul as stinking and as unnatural as we perceive vomit to be.

What is it that is sinful about gluttony? We have already touched on this briefly when we noted that the gravity and even the content of the sin might vary depending on whether the relevant society is one of plenty or one of endemic and severe scarcity. The general moral regime would also alter the moral stakes and the moral content of gluttony: for instance, in rigid ascetic communities gluttony might be more of a temptation than pride, lust more than wrath. The idea that gluttony is sinful because it involves an unjust distribution of a necessity for the maintenance of life is rarely posed as the central moral issue of gluttony even in the Middle Ages. Still it figures in the Middle Ages and more then than now. But even in modern times we are asked to consider our own plenteous consumption in the face of the starvation of others. The difference is that in Dives's world he literally ate in the face of Lazarus; Lazarus was in his sight. We, on the other hand, must exercise a bit of imagination to see the starving as we eat. The walls that ensure our privacy and provide the basis for no small amount of our complacency allow us also to imagine the starving as less repulsive and more pathetically deserving of our attention than their immediate presence would tend to make them; but the same immured privacy also lets us simply tune them out by turning off the evening news.

Dives's remedial action is easy and obvious: he should have fed and cared for Lazarus. Ours is less easy and obvious because the other's suffering takes place at a distance and is mediated via impersonal markets and international charitable organizations that promise to translate our cash into food at some distant point out of our sight. When I was a child my teachers told me to think of the poor starving Koreans and to eat everything on the plate of my government-subsidized hot lunch. Even to a first-grade kid it seemed absurd to think that eating what revolted me helped relieve starving Koreans. There are several layers of irony that turn the puritanical slogan of waste not, want not, into a counsel as much in favor of gluttony as against it.

There were other grounds, recited by both medieval and classical writers, of gluttony's viciousness and danger. Surely gluttony destroyed the soul, but it also destroyed the body, the very object to which the glutton was so devoted. Gluttony was unhealthy:

> Hereof procedeth the vomit and the stone
> And other sickness many more than one.[27]

If arguments urging charity toward others fell on deaf ears, and arguments directed toward postmortem eternity were too remote to impel compliance, the preacher had recourse to naked and present self-interest. The Anglican homilist tried to terrorize his listeners into compliance by noting the sudden deaths that cometh with banqueting. Excess generates unnatural heat making the body sluggish and "unfit to serve either God or man." And the glutton gets more negatives than positives from his food: "Except God give strength to nature to digest, so that we may take profit by [our foods,], either shall we filthily vomit them up again, or else shall they lie stinking in our bodies, as in a loathsome sink or channel."[28]

The preacher pulls no punches here; he seeks to quell appetite by reminding the glutton just how his body transforms his delectables into the quintessence of the disgusting: vomit and feces. Food thus becomes its own punishment, its own hell on earth. One writer even suggests that the glutton should be punished as a suicide:

> We do nothing but fatten our souls to Hellfire. Our bodies we bombast and ballast with engorging diseases. Diseases shorten our days, therefore whosoever englutteth himself, is guilty of his own death and damnation.[29]

The devil, of course, was no slouch either and he used arguments from health to prompt gluttony. Fasts will weaken you, you must keep your body's health for holiness. Says the devil: "Don't eat for the delight of the body, but to serve God the better; thou shalt keep thy strength to serve God; that's what David says."[30]

We, like those premodern preachers, make gluttony a matter of health, more so than they did. For us it is a major argument; for them it was a minor one. Some of the viciousness they find in gluttony strikes us as strange. Gluttony not only wastes what others could more profitably use; it also wastes your own estate. The fear was not just ill corporeal health, but poverty, even as late as the early eighteenth century:

> Fat pamper'd Porus, eating for Renown,
> In soups and sauces melts his manors down
> Regardless of his heirs, with mortgag'd Lands,
> Buys hecatombs of fish and ortolans.[31]

This concern is a corollary to the economic point made earlier regarding a regime of severe scarcity. Sumptuous fare was expensive. And recall that gluttony is always more than a matter of quantity; it is also about delicacy and rarity, exquisiteness and voluptuousness of the palate. Robert Burton notes in *The Anatomy of Melancholy* a perverse psychological verity that "those things please most which cost most. The dearest cates[32] are best" (I.ii.ii.ii). And as we have seen, pride entered the fray to up the ante too, because how much you spent determined your rank in this gluttonous potlatch.

Gluttony is vicious because in some economies it is a form of homicide, because it is also unhealthy and so a form of suicide, and because it wastes one's own goods, risking poverty for oneself and securing it for one's heirs. Some of these grounds strike us as more compelling than others, but they were all makeweights in the moralist's argument against gluttony. The true ground of gluttony's sinfulness was that it, along with lust, was a sin of what was once known as Security, that is, culpable negligence in the ordering of one's own system of values. Thomas Nashe, writing in the late sixteenth century, puts it best: Security is "forgetting mortalitie; it is a kind of Alchymical quintessensing of a heaven out of earth."[33] These are the people whose God is their belly, the ones who drove the flinty St. Paul to tears.[34]

In a moral order that sets great stock by what it calls the spiritual, the glutton poses against it not just general corporeality, but the most vulgar and unseemly corporeality: not the arms and legs, not muscle, but organ meat, the gut. The gut should never be an end in itself; it should always figure subserviently as a means that enables other nobler, less embarrassing portions of the body and soul to thrive. The belly is there to serve the spiritual, the intellectual, and the productive working body that tills the soil. In the Christian scheme the glutton's sin was close to apostasy; it was infidelism. Paul chose his metaphors with a purpose: these people substituted their guts for God. The belly is more than a false god. It constitutes a special affront; it mocks God in a way His other competitors do not. Some false gods at least demand heroism, sacrifice, or the denial of self-serving concerns about one's own salvation.[35] But the glutton's god was his own pampered gut; by thus incarnating God in such a low-status organ he also reduced himself to mouth, gut, and anus, a mere tube fueling a feel-good machine.

This was no minor sin in the Christian scheme, at least as Paul would have it. True, pride set oneself up against God, thus in fact its special grievousness; but pride took one's virtue, one's glory, one's might and main, one's gifts and achievements seriously and valued them. Pride did not deny the spirit. Rather it challenged God by posing an indomitable human spirit against the demands of the Divine One for obedience and subservience; gluttony simply sets up the alimentary canal as the end, an end that sees us finally reduced to fat, sated flesh lolling in a viscous, oozing spiritless life soup, to an eternal recurrence of feeding, excreting, rotting, and generating. (To be sure, pride has its vulgar side too, but the simplification still captures a certain truth about the difference between pride and gluttony.)

Yet didn't Christianity ask for the trouble it got from gluttony, at least once the doctrine of transubstantiation was made dogma in 1215? Christianity, after all, featured the mouth and the alimentary canal in the central mystery of the faith: the Eucharist. This is not a twentieth-century secularist making a fanciful connection. The faithful made it seven centuries ago. A certain style of mystical devotion that focused its intensity on the Eucharist used images of glutting, sating, and eating to describe taking in the wafer and wine. There were, in other words, gluttons for God in the multiple senses "for" can have in that phrase: they wanted to serve him (there is even a pun here) and eat him. Consider this thirteenth-century hagiography describing one Mary of Oignies, a mystic who was especially devoted to the Eucharist:

> the holy bread strengthened her heart; the holy wine inebriated her, rejoicing her mind; the holy body fattened her. . . . Indeed she felt all delectation and all savor of sweetness in receiving it, not just within her soul but even in her mouth. . . .[36]

There is a wit in this kind of devotion. It takes the sin of gluttony and consciously seeks to spiritualize it, enlisting it and the gut in the service of God.

The passage about Mary of Oignies reminds us that gluttony is more than just chowing down and glutting to the point of sickness. There is more to it than the belly; there is also the palate. That Mary was fatted by eating Jesus was only part of the pleasure; it was also that he tasted good, "all delectation and all savor of sweetness." Gluttony has two chief forms that at times raise demands inconsistent with each other. One form is about ingesting excessive quantities; the other about excessive refinements as to quality. The quantity/quality distinction was there in Gregory the Great's taxonomy of gluttony back in the sixth century: not just eating too much, but also eating too daintily. We may even suppose that when Paul spoke tearfully against those who made their bellies their god he did not mean to exclude those who make the palate their god. The belly metaphor seems big enough to include the devotees of quality as well as those of quantity. Here the psychology and physiology of alimentation help make the case. Consider that taste alone is seldom, if ever, a pleasure entirely unto itself. If it were, dieting would hardly be a challenge. The fact is that there is little pleasure in tasting a good taste only to have to spit it out before swallowing. The pleasure of a good taste remains to a large extent inchoate unless the substance bearing the good taste is swallowed. The bulimic helps make the point by swallowing first, thus completing the pleasure cycle of ingestion and only then putting the process into reverse. Even gum chewing requires the swallowing of the saliva generated by the minty or fruity taste or there is no pleasure.[37] No swallowing, and instead of pleasure we experience frustration and disappointment. An analogy with *coitus interruptus* suggests itself, but in fact not swallowing good-tasting food might be even more displeasuring. So it is that the belly is a necessary condition to the pleasure of the palate.

Does the glutton who lives to gorge on large amounts have values more out of whack than the glutton whose chief goal in life is the experience of subtle delectations and rarefied pleasurings of the palate? Is one more a sinner than the other? More shallow? Do they offend in the same way? Both, it seems, can be accused of finding in fleshly sensation the desired end of their existence, and in this sense both have equally given themselves over to a false and very corporeal god. But there has been a historical ebb and flow between which style of gluttony—the quantitative or the qualitative—was most offensive, although both always merited the scorn of the moralist.

Hume makes the following claim:

> The more men refine upon pleasure, the less they indulge in excesses of any kind; because nothing is more destructive to true pleasure than such excesses. One may safely affirm, that the Tartars are oftener guilty of beastly gluttony, when they feast on their dead horses, than European courtiers with all their refinements of cookery.[38]

Hume introduces the idea that the civilizing process bears a powerful relation to the nature of particular vices, especially, as here, to gluttony. Hume, of course, in this passage is making the case for the virtues of refinement as these are secured by the civilizing process. In brief, that process led to an increase in sensitivities of disgust and embarrassment and an internalization of norms of bodily decorum. You were no longer to fart, pick your nose, piss, or defecate in the presence of others. Food was to be eaten decorously without slurping or burping.[39] By Hume's time you ate with a fork, not with your hands; it was barbaric to wipe your hands or blow your nose on the table cloth or to spit on the floor. Just two centuries earlier these behaviors were possible without calling any special attention to yourself. We already witnessed the earliest stages of this process when Langland opposed the privatizing of eating, preferring instead the distributional advantages of large riotous feasts where bones were tossed to the dogs and to the poor. That very limiting of eating to smaller, more intimate, and less festive groupings helped in part to do the work of turning Tartars into courtiers, although at some cost in social and psychic dislocation.

But is Hume right? He admits that gluttony is not eliminated by refinement. He seems to concede that European courtiers are gluttons even with their refinements. More correctly he admits that courtly gluttony is a function of these refinements. What he is arguing is that the European courtly obsession with delicate cuisine is not as gluttonous as are some Tartars chomping on their dead horses. Gluttonous it still is, but, in his estimation, paler in comparison. So what precisely is the ground of comparison? At first glance it appears to be merely a matter of quantities of food consumed, the notion of excess being more attracted to quantity than to quality. What the Tartars lack in culinary refinement, they make up for in bulk, and that very bulk makes them more gluttonous than the courtier. The cleverness of Hume's imagery reinforces this. He makes us see a hoard of Tartars each eating one newly skinned, barely roasted horse that was either ridden to death or shot out from under him, "beastly" gluttons in more than one sense. The courtier on the other hand eats delicate morsels delicately, each morsel bearing no resemblance to the ingredients that made it up. But is there no excess there? Excess there surely is, but it is not of bulk so much as in fleshly sensation, the courting of fleshly delight. What refinement succeeds in doing is not eliminating gluttony but doing just what refinement is supposed to do: make the pleasure more exquisite, but no less sinful, no less a confusion of the means for the proper end. Refinement proceeds by a kind of condensation in which more punch is packed in a smaller package.

But it is not just a matter of an excess of titillation and delectation. Hume knows, I suspect, although he is suppressing the knowledge for the purpose of making his anti-Puritanical point, that there can also be an excess of refinement itself, not just of the delicious and voluptuous sensations it makes possible. Excesses in refinement might be a contradiction in terms, because true refinement should also know how to regulate itself, how never to engender vulgarity, how always to be decorous even if that means compromising certain rules of refinement in the interests of its spirit and style. Yet refinement seems, inevitably, to foster the production of its own brand of vulgarity and excess that is both engendered by it and parasitical to it: for example, foppery, gourmetism, and certain kinds of priggishness.

It is thus not altogether clear that excesses of refinement can't generate disgusts in the observer almost as great as the bestial excesses of devouring huge quantities without coming up for air. Compare for instance a thick-necked, pot-bellied man stuffing the contents of a heaping plate of barbecue into his pink and sweating face as he gropes for another beer, to a slender elegant man with an Anglophilic accent, the kind affected by the transatlantic-liner set in 1930s movies, sniffing his wine glass and pronouncing the year and the vintage to be superb. Although not pink in the face, he extends his pinky as he takes a decorous sip, raising his eyes as if in devotion to God. Both disgust most of us. And depending on the social class or the body type of the observer, it is not at all clear who disgusts more. Both manifest ineffable shallowness, even though the shallowness has distinctly different styles. Both engage in a kind of unseemliness, and unseemliness is generally a matter of excess. One style is gendered vulgar masculine, the other vulgar feminine; one low class, the other pretentiously claiming for itself the superiority of expertise and highness, but often taking on the style of an unintended parody of highness. And both make their gut their god, although the second, having adopted the idiom of excessive refinement, has the palate serving as his gut's vicar on earth.

Both men demonstrate that there is something very dangerous about eating. It is hard not to offend God or your fellow man or woman when you do it. And God and humanity seem to be taking offense at roughly the same thing: the unseemliness of gratifying bodily urges. Eating is like other necessary bodily functions: dangerous in the extreme and best done out of sight. In fact the Brahmins have pretty much adopted this course.[40] Like sex, eating must be hemmed in with all kinds of rituals and rules precisely because the process is so likely to prompt disgust when viewed by others. Watch with a detached eye as someone, even a well-mannered someone, eats. It is not a thing of beauty. But if skilled we can at least make feeding ourselves relatively inoffensive, when, again as in sex, we agree to put ourselves at mutual risk so as not to make ourselves so vulnerable to the gaze of a noneating other.

The civilizing process, the process that made eating riskier than it already was, shifted the emphasis in gluttony from a matter of excessive amounts to a matter of excessive concentrated sensation. It was the civilizing process that in no small part helped make the very civilized sensibility of David Hume possible. And at the same time advancing refinement shifted the moral focus of gluttony from a disgust prompted by the perversion of proper spiritual values or by consuming more than your just share amidst starving Lazaruses to a disgust for bad manners, for looking vulgar as you ate. In either case, unseemliness was at issue. But refinement held the seeds of its own undoing. Refined people may demand refined cuisine, but refined cuisine might taste so good, so much better than dead horses, that it could work to prompt its refined consumers to excesses of quantity in the old gluttonous style. Hume, we might note, was quite portly and appeared to enjoy his refined cuisine in abundance. No wonder Hume's moral order rescued gluttons from the third circle of hell where Dante had them wallowing in the mire like hogs. Hume, matching Christ's harrowing of hell, led forth the gluttons to a new order. If they were vulgar gluttons, their punishment was to be banishment from refined company, but if they indulged sensation in ways that the new refinement anticipated and supported, then, as long as they did not do so to the exclusion of other virtues, they were to be excused for an eternity.

I confess that I have been exaggerating somewhat in order to capture what is merely a shift in emphasis. The core unseemliness of gluttony remained fairly constant through time, and it was largely Paul's version of unseemliness that governed. The pursuit of cheap thrills, of mere feel-good sensation was sinfully shallow. Even Hume admitted that the vice of luxury—lust and gluttony—is vicious "when it engrosses all a man's expense, and leaves no ability for such acts of duty and generosity as are required by his situation and fortune."[41] When gluttony and lust undermined benevolence and amiability, they were still for Hume vices. But like the gluttony of the classical and premodern moralist, the spiritual bankruptcy of Hume's gluttony bore an unseemly connection to the risk of worldly bankruptcy.

Philology, the words people used to talk about gluttony and excesses in fleshly and alimentary matters, also provides evidence of gluttony's transformation through time. Words like *delicacy, gourmand,* and *luxury* moved from distinctly pejorative senses to fairly neutral ones. *Delicacy* initially meant the quality of being addicted to sensual pleasure and encompassed both lust and gluttony, but mostly gluttony. Thomas Nashe (in the sixteenth century), for instance, discussed under the general heading of Delicacy, gluttony, luxury (meaning lust), sloth, and security. Delicacy was the excessive immersion in bodily pleasure—especially that of the palate—to the exclusion of all else. But then slowly the notion of delicacy got caught up in the civilizing process; it got refined. Instead of referencing sin, it now referenced a delicacy of taste, a sensitivity to the elegant, to the pleasing, to refined and subtle sensation, so that from its immoral beginnings in gorging, it ends, by the time Hume is writing in the first half of the eighteenth century, marking feelings of modesty, the sense of propriety, and a delicate regard for the feelings of others.

Once delicacy comes to operate in the terrain of refinement rather than sin, however, that very refinement starts to spin off pejorative senses again—not, this time, pejorative in the old excessive style of gluttony, but in the new more refined one. Without quite giving up on the positive senses of refinement it had come to acquire, delicacy begins to be colored by an insinuation of excess of a different cast than its early gluttonous one. Its new excess is one of exquisite decadence, or of a kind of tender weakness and fragility that is gendered feminine. In other words, the history of the word *delicacy* tracks almost to a T the changes we noted above in the shift in gluttony as eating too much to the sin of caring too much about what you ate. Delicacy, like gluttony, got caught in the trammels of the increasing sensitivity to disgust and embarrassment that were part of the civilizing process.

*Gourmand* is less interesting, but it too moves from meaning glutton to meaning, by the middle of the eighteenth century, someone who has a refined expertise in food, a gourmet, before drifting back again toward gluttony. The history of the word *luxury* tells a similar story, with the emphasis, however, more on lust than on gluttony. It moved from being the proper word for what we call lust to meaning luxury as we know it—the general indulgence in costly and superfluous finery, including food. The move in each case is toward a "decriminalization" of gluttony, lessening its moral stakes, and then a subtle recriminalization of it at a lower level, reflecting again the drift from the unseemliness of quantity to the unseemliness of excessive concern with quality. What was once a masculine sin (in medieval portrayals of the sins, gluttony is masculine) becomes the effeminate excesses of fastidiousness, delicacy, and persnicketiness. The eighteenth century in many respects sees gluttony at its low point as a sin. The new form of the gluttony of quality, of hyperfastidiousness, was not, like the old gluttony of quantity, a sin of denying one's humanity in favor of hoglike bestiality; it had become the sin of a particular form of human shallowness annexed to vanity and pride. Yet unlike pride, it had its roots in the shallowness of purely physical pleasure.

If gluttony was less urgent as a matter for moralists in the eighteenth century, it was still of considerable political concern. Politics still paid homage to gluttony as sin; it became kind of a rallying cry in fact. When Marie Antoinette relegated the poor to their wretched cakes while she enjoyed refined multi-course dinners, these new Lazaruses in the Jacobin style were not so willing to trust God to deal with Marie as He had with Dives; nor, it should be added, did they trust Him to deal with themselves any better in the next life than He had in this one. So they made their earthly paradise by ensuring Marie got her hell right here. The lower orders, it seems, saw the consumption of refinement to be no less offensive than the consumption of barbaric and bestial excess. From their perspective, in other words, the transition from a gluttony of quantity to a fastidious gluttony of quality was too subtle to notice. Yet there was a difference. Marie conceded a lot more to the Parisian mob than Dives did to Lazarus. Production levels were higher; they at least had their gâteaux, unrefined though they may have been.

In the nineteenth and twentieth centuries gluttony continued to recognize two styles—the one of excessive quantity, the other of excessive concern with quality—but these were altered to accommodate an even more secular world. Gluttony still was a sin, and indeed a sin around which religiopolitical movements could rally. This time it was not food so much as drink, demon rum. Temperance movements made the mouth and the gullet the originators of moral and social offense. If revulsion and indignation at what and how the rich were *eating* fueled the riots of the Parisian poor, the thought of what and how much the poor were *drinking* revolted and terrified the middle classes and the rich. The temperance movement was a riot of the better-heeled, and in

America they succeeded in ruining conviviality for quite some time. In the Middle Ages no real distinction was made in the sinfulness of indulging drink rather than food; the poor had precious little of either. Class distinctions, however, helped give social and political stakes to the distinction between food and drink in matters of gluttony that was already beginning to be made, as we saw, by the late sixteenth century. It is only recently, that is post–World War II, that the food/drink distinction has ceased to matter much.

With increasing secularization, gluttony, in the second half of the twentieth century, was no longer the special provenance of the preacher or the moralist as we conventionally think of them. The new preacher was the doctor, the personal trainer, the dietitian, the aerobics instructor, shrinks for the body and shrinks for the mind; and preaching came to us in voiceovers in commercials, or in the mere sight of the models in them and other figures of desirability and beauty purveyed in art and mass media. Despite our post-Freudian obsession with sexuality, we, like our medieval forebears, put food before sex, except we gave a rather different meaning to the ordering. Eating for them meant festivity, jollity, conviviality, communion both sacred and profane, and then rolling in the hay (I am painting a cartoon here, but not an altogether false one). Food was its own pleasureful end, but it was also foreplay for the occasional lusty and lickerous frosting on the cake. They ate because it was desirable and generated sexual desire as a consequence; we strategize, count calories, worry, and undermine our pleasure in eating so as not to undo what little desirability we may be lucky enough to possess. *Food first then fornication* described for them the paradigmatic ordering of pleasure; for us the same motto describes a regime of mortification of the flesh for an overrated payoff.

The moral discourse of contemporary gluttony has rather different emphases than earlier styles. We speak of eating disorders and addictions that are classified as illness rather than as sin. But in our culture of health in which the state of one's body is felt to govern largely the state of one's soul, we have simply attached sin to illness so that in the end we hold people to *moral* account for their illnesses. The alcoholic, the anorexic, the bulimic, the obese do not become unblamable just because they are cared for by doctors and psychologists rather than confessors and preachers. Of course, those who have eating disorders that make them fat rather than thin fare much worse in the moral calculus, much in the way a calorie of sugar from fruit is *morally* superior to a Twinkie calorie. We are thus more likely to excuse the anorexic than the obese, to make her somewhat less culpable, partly in deference to her tender years, partly in deference to her sex, but mostly because we are not as revolted by her disorder until its terminal stages. She also benefits from our willingness to allow the thin tragic possibility; the fat, in contrast, are relegated almost without exception to comedy, farce, and the grotesque.

Bulimia, addictions, and binge eating are classic instances of gluttony. Anorexia is slightly more complex, but it captures all that the earlier moralists held to comprise the sin of gluttony. The alimentary canal takes over; it dominates one's life; thoughts of quantity become all consuming. The belly still stands as god even if it has a minus sign in front of it. Medieval moralists understood this also. They discussed fasting under the heading of gluttony, and while they approved of reasonable abstinence within recognized and regulated religious ritual, they blamed excessive fasting as unhealthy both to body and soul. Moreover, they suspected the compulsive and aggressive faster of hypocrisy, of putting on shows of sanctity: "thou fasteth much in men's sight in order to be lean and pale, to seem ghostly [that is, spiritual]. Thou art an hypocrite."[42]

Anorexia and bulimia show that modern forms of gluttony are distinctly gendered. Both these disorders are almost exclusively the provenance of teenage and college-age women. Although it has been suggested that the occasionally suicidal fasting of certain medieval women saints had all the trappings of anorexia, the ideal of abstinence and mortification of the flesh made such behaviors less exclusively female than they are today, even if women then pushed themselves more toward self-destruction than did males. In our age, the styles of gluttony track class and gender divisions. Fat is as consistent a marker of lower-class membership as there is for both sexes; it may even be a better predictor than skin color. The fat, really fat, are not likely to be as educated, as wealthy, or as from California as the thin. Class predicts rather well which gluttons will be gluttons of quantity and which will be gluttons of quality.

Gluttony occupies the extremes—Rabelaisian glutting as well as anorexia and saintly mortification of the flesh—because at either extreme the spirit has been turned over to the alimentary. Our only hope is the mean, the dull middle in which reasonableness governs. Even here we run into trouble. Reasonableness may once have been the answer, although we may surely quibble on that point; but in a culture obsessed with health, longevity, and beauty, reasonableness sounds less like the advice of the moralist or theologian than of the doctor. The middle ground is no longer the region in which the spirit can thrive freed from the body's control; it is the very ground on which alimentary obsessions are claimed to produce the best results for fleshly pleasures and ends. Perversely, after being down but not out in the mid-eighteenth century, gluttony has arisen to reaffirm the place it held on the first extant list of the capital sins some sixteen hundred years ago. Gluttony now seems to be working mostly in the service of pride, yet so much of modern pride is consumed by gluttony that it is not always quite clear which vice is really bringing home the bacon. *Gula vincit omnia.*

## *REMEDIA GULAE* (THE REMEDIES OF GLUTTONY)

Medieval tracts devoted to the vices and virtues often follow their detailed and loving descriptions of the vices with much briefer sections setting forth remedies for them. The remedies are briefer because they do not engage the literary talents of the writer as intensely. No wonder: vices give us a rich array of behaviors; they are the stuff of good stories. Remedies for disorders, moral or physical, on the other hand, are just advice, and advice doesn't have the interesting narrative possibility that vice does. For gluttony, one is to be temperate and keep one's faith where it belongs. One is not to worship the belly or in the homilist's words be a "beastly belly slave."[43] That's it.

My remedy will not be another diet plan either in the fashion of these tracts or of its modern successors. In the short space that remains I wish to talk about certain systemic remedies that help work against gluttony, which if they don't quite rehabilitate the glutton surely punish him. We might divide these remedies into the physiological, like vomiting; the psychological, like accesses of disgust and remorse; and the social, like ostracism for being fat, for being a food snob, or for generally eating like a pig. I will focus on disgust and under its generous ambit touch on vomiting and excretion, with some small attention to remorse. I will consider the social remedies to have been adequately handled by remarks I have sprinkled throughout the essay up to this point.

Let us deal with remorse first. It is the rare glutton who does not repent of his indulgences. Falstaff, one of literature's premier gluttons—an "obscene greasy tallow catch," "a roasted Manningtree ox with the pudding in his belly," so fat that he "lards the lean earth as he walks along"[44]—is also Monsieur Remorse.[45] The diction of self-amendment is as much a part of his character as his wavering resolution to improve: "I'll repent and that suddenly, while I am in some liking."[46] The sins of the flesh, it seems, are the only ones that bring remorse and repentance naturally in their wake. Remorse, even guilt, come readily for our sins of lust and gluttony, but we are rather resistant to feeling remorse for our sins of pride, wrath, avarice, and sloth. Those are sins we have to be trained, hectored, exhorted, threatened, and disciplined into feeling bad about. Not so lust and gluttony for which remorse is an eager though unwelcome guest who enters via postcoital tristesse in the one case, and via nausea, hangover, or the mere sense of leaden satiation in the other. Gluttony and lust punish us physically, and this seems to be a much more reliable trigger for remorse than the more attenuated triggerings of remorse in the other sins. It is from gluttony or its alcohol variant that the public remorseful confessional style of AA and the twelve-step phenomenon got their start, not from pride or anger. Pride never lets us down when it is justified, when we really are better than those we compete with. Anger lets us down on occasion and when it does we feel remorse; but it can also yield the sweetest of pleasures, though no less sinful, as when it ends in delicious revenge.

If gluttony prompts remorse, it only does so because it had first elicited disgust. Disgust is a very complex sentiment, and it is ultimately charged with preventing or punishing those deeds that make us gluttons. First, it governs our relations to eating, not only what we eat, how we eat, and how much but also to the two disgust substances that are a direct consequence of (over)eating: vomit and feces. Second, it processes our view of others as they eat. And third, it governs our responses to the long-term consequences of gluttony: fat and bodily decay. Disgust does much more. In addition to providing the vehicle for our ambivalence toward the viscous ooze that is life, generation, rot, and regeneration, it patrols the boundaries that separate us from others, and it does some rather respectable work as a moral sentiment. Our moral possibility would be much poorer if we lacked disgust for the vices of cruelty, hypocrisy, foolishness, and general moral sliminess.[47]

Disgust has two main sub-types which though they can on occasion collapse into each other are still distinguishable. One type works to prevent any indulgence at all, not just overindulgence. It often works so as to keep us from fulfilling unconscious desires. This is basically the Freudian story of repression. The reason I do not sleep with Mom or Sis is because the thought revolts me. Disgust does both the repressing and is the consequence of successful repression. If there were no such desire, then disgust would be unnecessary since there would be no threatened breach to patrol against. This type of disgust also keeps us from eating certain things we may want to ingest: again in the Freudian story, these would be the forbidden delectables of infancy, like feces. Disgust of this sort gives force and soul to the classification of some foods as inherently disgusting, that is, those foods we deem polluting or defiling. Here too disgust, ideally, should nip desire in the bud.[48] Take the lament of a would-be glutton in the early sixteenth century, chagrined to find the fare he has waited for too disgusting to enjoy. The cheese is "full of maggots," the eggs "half-hatched," and the vessels in which the drink is served are "lately taken from some sink." Be advised that "sink" back then referred to a cesspool or pit for sewage:

> And in such vessel drink shalt thou often time,
> Which in the bottom is full of filth and slime,
> And of that vessel thou drinkest oft iwis [for sure]
> In which some states or dames late did piss.[49]   [states = lords]

The other main type of disgust responds to very conscious desires. In the first type of disgust the object—whether it is food as in gluttony or the mere thought of another's body or bodily discharges and odors as in the sin of lust—revolts us right from the start. The first disgust operates by trying to prevent imbibing in the first place, the second by punishing excessive imbibement. In the second type the object beckons and we respond with unambivalent desire. We leap right in and go at it. It is only after full immersion in the sensual delights that the second disgust kicks in. This is the disgust of surfeit which arises as a consequence of too much pleasure; its connection with gluttony is obvious. It is this disgust that is one of the chief curses of the human condition, threatening as it does to blight big pleasures by introducing ambivalence to once unambivalent desire. (The first type, however, may be considered one of the chief blessings of the human condition, animating our world with the truly and often enticingly forbidden.) In this way the disgust of surfeit begins to merge with the first type of disgust, which works to prohibit any sampling at all.

Vomiting, for instance, can be a powerful deterrent to finding pleasure again in certain foods. The vile stuff coming up bears just enough similarity and recognizability to the desirable stuff that went down to provide us with desire-killing memories for that kind of food.[50] Freud posited a loving relationship with our own feces, a kind of pride of production. No one has thought to make a similar claim for vomit. There is something unnatural about it; it reverses the forces of nature, forcing up what should go down. It denigrates and disparages all it comes into contact with, shamefully constraining the mouth to imitate an anus, which is always disgusting. Moreover, while we cannot avoid smelling our excrement, vomiting ups the ante: we can neither avoid smelling it nor *tasting* it. Vomit is a powerful sanction which can terrorize people into moderation and into refraining from certain excesses. The parents who change vile diapers with nary a thought must still steel themselves to clean up the vomit of their sick child. Even dogs, according to Langland, showed some discernment with regard to human vomit. They may have returned to their own as Proverbs claimed, but they would not touch the vomit of an allegorized Glutton. When Glutton coughs up a load in the lap of his drinking pal we are told:

> There is not so hungry a hound in Hertfordshire
> Darest lap up that leaving so unlovely it smelled.[51]

Yet some learn to survive vomit's vileness. Bulimics seek it out, and Romans even had vomitoria so as not to let fullness ruin the feast. In fact, many foods and especially drinks survive the shamefulness of vomiting to be indulged again. The disgust of surfeit need not be accompanied by the physical sensations of nausea or vomiting. All gluttons would be bulimics if that were the case and there would also be many fewer gluttons. Mostly the price the glutton pays is a disgust that is felt as a leaden sense of satiation, coupled with vague intimations of defilement, contamination, or pollution that can yield a kind of mini-shame or mini-panic about how to restore one's purity.

The two types of disgust in a rough way map on to the two main types of gluttony. The disgust of initial prohibition is the disgust that informs the food-snobbism of the gourmet. This disgust is the disgust that provides the psychological energy behind refinement. It is what keeps us from being Tartars munching on dead mares. This finely honed sense of disgust constitutes what we more politely think of as our sense of discernment; it seamlessly connects our knowledge and feelings about what is suitable to eat, how it is to be acceptably prepared and served, and how it should be eaten in a seemly way. This type of disgust, when appropriately modulated, is what makes for a person of taste. When excessive, it makes for fastidiousness and prissiness. When insufficiently sensitive, it makes for boorishness and vulgarity. True, without this type of disgust we would be less repressed. Civilization, so the Freudian story goes, fosters discontents. And one of these discontents is small portions or even no portions at all (as in the case of Mom and Sis) since so much has become disgusting.

The disgust of surfeit, on the other hand, is linked hand-in-glove with the common gluttony of excessive quantity. It punishes for each overimbibement, but never quite enough to prevent frequent recidivism. The disgust of refinement, of initial prohibition, would like us to find excessive quantity a matter for initial refusal, but, alas, our wills are weak. And the disgust of surfeit must be called in to punish our excesses when our breeding was insufficient to keep us from being pigs. Human, all too human.

Disgust, and to a lesser extent the remorse that it fuels, are just about all we have to oppose our gluttonous and fleshly desires. Appeals to pride of appearance and to pride of strength and vigor—that is, appeals to health—ultimately derive their effective energy from the disgust they are seeking to avoid: disgust with fat, ugliness, decay, flaccidity, and the uncleanness we feel that excess visits upon us. Only fear and cowardice, the engines of our pathetic desires to live longer than decorum suggests we should, can rival disgust as a sovereign remedy for gluttony—but then only for the gluttony of excess, not for the gluttony of refinement. If disgust at ourselves is not sufficient to the task of keeping our wills in line with regard to quantity, or if it is simply not activated as when our gluttony is one of quality, then we must rely on the disgust of others for us to do the ugly work of correction. The disgust and contempt we elicit in others who observe us "fressing," or who are revolted by the pretensions of our foodsnobbism, just might succeed in shaming us into

adopting the mean. But these are fond thoughts. That which is prohib-
ited because it tastes too good acquires by virtue of the very prohibition
the allure of the forbidden. To the attraction of the sensation of tastiness
is added the thrill of breaching a prohibition when we sin by imbibing.
Gluttony, despite the fat and disgust that attends it, is its own attraction
precisely because it is a sin. Would there were such thrills in store for us
in the virtue of temperance.

## NOTES

1. From "The Glutton," vv. 9–16, William Combe (1742–1823), *The English Dance of Death* (London: R. Ackermann, 1815), 68.

2. So impossible is it for us to conceive of Hamlet fat that, when Gertrude
declares him "fat and scant of breath" during the duel with Laertes (5.2.290),
editors have come to the rescue with glosses to show that fat meant sweaty and
out of shape, but manifestly not fat: see Harold Jenkins's spirited note in his
edition of *Hamlet* (New York: Routledge, 1981), 568–69.

3. "Of Refinement in the Arts," in *Essays, Moral, Political and Literary,* based
on 1777 ed., ed. Eugene F. Miller (Indianapolis: Liberty Fund, 1985), 268. Enthusiasm has here its early sense of religious enthusiasm referring to the ecstasies
of divine possession and the kinds of fanaticism and self-assertions that resulted
from the belief in such possession.

4. Reported in Mary Pipher, *Reviving Ophelia: Saving the Selves of Adolescent
Girls* (New York: Ballantine, 1994), 184.

5. Evagrius of Pontus (d. *c.* 400); see Morton Bloomfield, *The Seven Deadly
Sins* (Lansing: Michigan State College Press, 1952), 59–60.

6. I John 2:16. See Lester K. Little, "Pride Goes before Avarice: Social
Change and the Vices in Latin Christendom," *American Historical Review* 76
(1971), 16–49, at 21.

7. Guillaume Perrault's *Summa de vitiis et virtutibus* (thirteenth century) follows the Cassianic order beginning with gluttony; see Bloomfield 124.

8. *Canterbury Tales,* "Pardoner's Tale," vv. 498–504; cause first = first cause;
boght, aboght = redeemed. I am committing what I consider a grievous sin in
supplying modern spelling, where possible, for the Middle English forms. I have
also taken the liberty of normalizing some early modern spellings too, although
the original forms should not cause too much trouble, they will undoubtedly
trouble some readers enough to justify my crime.

9. Quoted in Aquinas, *Summa Theologica* 2a2æ. 148, 3.

10. "Sermon against Gluttony and Drunkennesse," in *Homilies appointed to be*

*read in churches in the time of Queen Elizabeth I, 1547–1571,* ed. Mary Ellen Rickey and Thomas B. Stroup (Gainesville, Fla.: Scholars' Facsimiles & Reprints, 1968), 68.

11. *Summa Theologica* 2a2æ. 148, 3.

12. St. Augustine, *Confessions* x. 31, trans. R. S. Pine-Coffin (Harmondsworth: Penguin, 1961).

13. *Summa Theologica* 2a2æ. 148, 5.

14. Humphrey Sydenham, *Sermons upon solemn occasions* (1637), 106.

15. See *Oxford English Dictionary* s.v. lickerous and lecherous.

16. See Rom Harré and Robert Finlay-Jones, "Emotion Talk Across Times," *The Social Construction of Emotions,* ed. Rom Harré (Oxford: Basil Blackwell, 1986), 220–33.

17. See *The Book of Vices and Virtues,* ed. W. Nelson Francis, Early English Text Society O. S. No. 217 (London: Oxford University Press, 1942), 52.

18. Alexander Barclay (1475?–1552), "The Second Eclogue of the Miseries of Courtiers," vv. 821–24, 829–30, in *The Eclogues of Alexander Barclay,* ed. Beatrice White. Early English Text Society, O. S. No. 175 (London: Oxford University Press, 1928), 51–106. See also *Piers Plowman* B 13.25–110 for a powerful example of envy and indignation for the sumptuous fare hypocritical friars claim for themselves as they preach of patient poverty.

19. *Piers Plowman* B 10.57; the alliteration shows that the initial "g" of gnaw was pronounced (c. 1370). See the delightful treatment of the oily friar in Chaucer's "Summoner's Tale" who discourses on the virtues of the fasting regimen of friars as he sups sumptuously at some townsman's board.

20. *Piers Plowman* B 10.96–102.

21. "General Prologue," v. 345.

22. *Jacob's Well: An Englisht Treatise on the Cleansing of Man's Conscience,* ed. Arthur Brandeis, Early English Text Society, O. S. 115 (London: Kegan Paul, Trench, Trübner, 1900), 143.

23. *Piers Plowman* B 1.32–33.

24. Thomas Nashe, *Christs Teares over Jerusalem* (London: James Roberts, 1593), 76v.

25. On the genealogy of this tradition of gluttony see R. F. Yeager, "Aspects of Gluttony in Chaucer and Gower," *Studies in Philology* 81 (1984), 42–55.

26. See Chaucer, "The Pardoner's Tale," vv. 463–76; see also Barclay, "Second Eclogue," vv. 538–92. *The Book of Vices and Virtues* (53–55) makes the point that whereas God in Holy Church makes the blind sighted, the halt whole, the insane sane; in the tavern the devil does the opposite.

27. Barclay, "Second Eclogue," vv. 627–28.

28. *Homilies* 98.

29. Nashe, *Christs Tears* 76v.

30. *The Book of Vices and Virtues* 51.
31. Thomas Warton (1688?–1745), "The Glutton," vv. 1–4, in *Poems on Several Occasions* reproduced from the edition of 1748 (New York: Facsimile Text Society, 1930), 177–79.
32. Choice fare, delicacies, dainties.
33. *Christs Teares* 75v.
34. Philippians 3:18–19.
35. I suppose we could imagine a glutton fighting a duel with the cook who ruined his pâté but he would not be doing so as a glutton if he did.
36. Cited in Caroline Walker Bynum, "Women Mystics and Eucharistic Devotion in the Thirteenth Century," in *Fragmentation and Redemption: Essays on Gender and the Human Body in Medieval Religion* (New York: Zone Books, 1992), 119.
37. There are some small exceptions like pleasure in the tastes of tobacco as smoke or as chewing tobacco. There still is ingestion in each case, but it is not effected in the gut and not by swallowing. One of the many vulgarities of chaw is the perversity of raising expectoration to a pleasure on a par with swallowing.
38. "On Refinement in the Arts," *Essays* 271–72.
39. See Norbert Elias, *The History of Manners*, Vol. 1 of *The Civilizing Process,* trans. Edmund Jephcott (New York: Urizen, 1978).
40. See Louis Dumont, *Homo Hierarchicus* (Chicago: University of Chicago Press, 1970); and Mary Douglas, *Purity and Danger* (London: Routledge and Kegan Paul, 1966).
41. "On Refinement in the Arts," 279.
42. *Jacob's Well,* 143.
43. "Sermon against Gluttony and Drunkennesse," 97.
44. I Henry IV, II.iv.227, 452; II.ii.109.
45. I.ii.116.
46. III.iii.4.
47. I am trying to condense here, and very inadequately, some few points made at length with a number of others in my *The Anatomy of Disgust* (Cambridge: Harvard University Press, 1997).
48. Space requires that I presently ignore the central paradox of disgust that makes the disgusting also alluring or that makes the breach of prohibitions that also may be backed by disgust rules offer the prospect of complex pleasures.
49. Barclay, "Second Eclogue," vv. 753, 761, 638–42.
50. The vomiting need not have been caused by surfeiting. My five-year-old boy's favorite food was Caesar salad until a very bad stomach flu struck him one hour after he consumed the equivalent of three adult-sized portions of it. He has lost what was for him one of the purest pleasures in his young life.
51. *Piers Plowman* B 5.356–57.

# 2

## PRIDE AND IDENTITY

### Jerome Neu

How is it that pride has gone from being one of the traditional seven deadly sins to becoming, in recent decades, the banner under which social movements have declared their objectives (Black Pride, Gay Pride, and so on)? How are we to understand the shift from a theology of sin to a politics of self-assertion (and an accompanying psychology of self-esteem)? Is it simply that times have changed? That, God having died, attitudes have changed—so that what once was thought to precede a fall now seems a condition of rising? Or is it perhaps that the nature of pride is to be understood differently in the two contexts? There may be an inherent ambiguity in pride: associating it on the one hand with arrogance, conceit, egotism, and vanity, and on the other hand with self-respect, self-esteem, self-confidence, dignity. (On certain readings, these may *all* be seen as different kinds or degrees of self-love.) Thus at different times, different aspects of the nature of the emotion come to be given prominence. Or is the difference in the objects? One place to start is with the recognition that the object, and the subject, of the traditional sin was the individual. The social movements that argue for pride are concerned with groups. How do individual and group identity come together in pride?

### "WE'RE NUMBER 1!"

"We're number 1! We're number 1!" It is the ecstatic chant of fans around the world when their sports team wins. The shout has gone up

51

quite often in San Francisco in recent years from fans of the 49ers football team. But who exactly is the "we" that is claiming exalted status? It is most often not the players themselves. Their claim to victory and so status would seem straightforward enough. But what have the fans done to deserve credit? They have often watched the game (but is that necessary?) and cheered their heroes on to victory. Perhaps the cheers of encouragement do help (there is said to be a "home team advantage"). But if the watching is done through television, as it most often is, the cheers can hardly reach and encourage the players. So the causal contribution of the ecstatic fans to victory may be minimal. But even where it is great, some would doubt that cheering itself is enough. The "49er Faithful" is a group of long-term fans who resent the Johnny-come-latelies who jump on the winning bandwagon to claim the 49ers as their own. After all, the Faithful had done their cheering and buying of merchandise during the many fallow years before a string of victories made the team so immensely popular. So is length of commitment a condition of group membership, and therefore credit for (subgroup) achievement? Is the motive of commitment relevant? Does it matter whether a fan decides to attach his or her good wishes to only winning teams or sticks (more or less consistently) to the home or nearest local team? Is identification with a winning team simply a matter of individual choice at all?

Surely some aspects of our identity are fixed independently of what we think or would like to think. Thus we can be embarrassed *by* something our parents say, where we might just be embarrassed *for* a stranger (such as an actor who forgets his lines on stage when we are in the audience). Thus also we can be ashamed of something our country does, even if we are part of a vocal minority that actively opposes the policy. (This was the situation of many Americans during the Vietnam War; see Walsh.) For certain purposes, who we are is fixed by who others think we are. Their criteria are the relevant ones—though our endorsing and incorporating their perspective may also be crucial. (If we reject their perspective, we perhaps ought to be free of the consequent emotions.) If those around us take family membership to be determined by blood, and citizenship to be determined by place of birth or other factors not directly chosen or readily disavowable, then insofar as family membership or citizenship provides grounds for pride or shame, those emotions too can become independent of our actions and preferences.

Equally surely, some aspects of our identity depend on choices we

make and allegiances we adopt. Sports fans are notably self-selecting—
but as we have noted, there may be complications even there. The complications are especially obvious where the organization is more formal:
joining an organization may be voluntary, but acceptance may be uncer-
tain, and so membership may itself become a special source of pride.
This is true for colleges, clubs, gangs, fraternities, and many other
groups, including military organizations ("The Few, The Proud, The
Marines"). Even where a voluntary choice is essential to group membership, and to pride based on group membership, the reactions and other
conditions placed on our choice by others may be equally essential.

But the complications of choice in relation to group membership
and so individual identity are only a part of the picture. That they *are* a
part of the picture, we should be clear, is due to the internal structure of
pride. David Hume treats pride (like all passions) as a "simple and uniform impression" (THN, II, 277) that cannot be defined or analyzed
into parts. Nonetheless, he manages to bring out some of what should
be regarded as the conceptual conditions of pride (he himself mistakenly
regarded them as simply causal conditions and consequences). His general scheme treats pride as a pleasure of self-approval, such "that all
agreeable objects, related to ourselves, by an association of ideas and
of impressions, produce pride, and disagreeable ones, humility" (Hume
THN, II, 290ff.; see Neu 1977, Part I). He includes *closeness to self* among
the modifications or "limitations" to that scheme. According to Hume,
the agreeable object must be *closely* related to ourselves (otherwise only
"joy" and not pride is produced) and only to ourselves or at most to
ourselves and a few others (hence the comparative and competitive nature of pride). Again, while Hume mistook these conceptual constraints
for merely causal ones, a proper pride (here meaning a conceptually
coherent pride, not necessarily a morally justified one) must indeed depend on a suitably valuable object being suitably related to one. For
Hume, value was simply a matter of approval and disapproval, ultimately
traceable to reactions of pleasure and pain. We shall see that the contemporary politics of pride must depend on a different notion of value and
of what is valuable. And while individual identity was notoriously a
special problem within Hume's narrowly empiricist philosophy of mind,
tracing chains of credit back to a self must be problematic on any philosophy, at least so far as credit is taken to depend on group membership.

Relation to self is a conceptual condition of pride, and closeness to self is, inevitably, open to complication and challenge.


## PRIDE THE SIN

Christian *pride* has some connections with Classical *hubris* (and even Jewish *chutzpah*), but the Christian notion is wider than just insolence or defiance against the gods. Nonetheless, such defiance was what gave the sin its medieval preeminence. Pride was given first place (one might say, "pride of place") back in the seventh century in Gregory the Great's now-conventional list of seven deadly sins (Bloomfield 72–74). The arrogance of pride was for him the root of all evil, "the beginning of all sin" (Lyman 136). There is biblical ground for giving pride such primacy (Ecclesiasticus 10:15 in the Vulgate), though I Timothy 6:10 gives avarice the prize. (St. Thomas made one of his usual efforts to reconcile the texts [Bloomfield 88]). Pride isolates and alienates from both God and society; it is a form of self-satisfied and self-sufficient withdrawal (Fairlie 42). For a medieval world committed to discipline, hierarchy, and corporate order, this made it particularly heinous. As Bloomfield puts it, pride "is the sin of rebellion against God, the sin of exaggerated individualism" (75).

The negative view of pride that has carried over to our more individualistic times picks up on the arrogance and error associated with the earlier notion, though a modifier is sometimes added to spell out the problem: *false* pride is explicitly seen as based on false beliefs, just as *overweening* pride is by definition excessive. Must pride by its very nature fall into error and excess?

Pride is, in part, a sin of judgment, an intellectual deviation, involving bias in favor of one's self. The bias is of course motivated, so the defect is not purely intellectual. Spinoza's definition captures this aspect of pride quite precisely: "Pride is thinking more highly of oneself than is just, out of love of oneself" (*Ethics* III, Definitions of the Affects XXVIII). The source of pride in self-love makes clear its link to self-esteem (understood in a sense that allows for excess), as Spinoza puts it: "Pride is an effect or property of Self-love. Therefore, it can also be defined as Love of oneself, or Self-esteem, insofar as it so affects a man that he thinks more highly of himself than is just" (ibid.). Oddly to the modern mind, Spinoza argues, "There is no opposite of this affect. For no one, out of hate, thinks less highly of himself than is just." But today's many self-help psychologies that insist on self-love and self-esteem as a precondition for a happy and effective life assume that failures of self-love are pervasive. Spinoza's argument actually depends on a rather special point: that if you think you cannot do something, you *therefore* cannot do it, certainly you won't try, and (however self-defeating) you therefore cannot be underestimating your abilities, for your estimate and your abilities are conceptually (in this negative direction) linked. Spinoza goes on to acknowledge a number of ways in which a person can think less highly of himself than is just and describes the relevant affect as "despondency" ("as Pride is born of Self-esteem, so Despondency is born of Humility," which is a form of sadness [Definition XXIX, Exp.]). Whatever the relation of pride and humility (is humility a virtue or simply an opposing error of judgment?) and of pride and shame (there are grounds for regarding them as true emotional, if not moral, opposites), we should not too quickly follow Spinoza in building error into our definition of pride. As a matter of modern usage, while pride may sometimes indeed be *false* and *overweening,* that we speak of *wounded* pride in connection with various forms of humiliation shows pride can also be a matter of dignity and self-respect. Similarly, Adam Smith points out in his *The Theory of Moral Sentiments* that "We frequently say of a man that he is too proud, or that he has too much noble pride, ever to suffer himself to do a mean thing" (416). Spinoza himself tells us that "Self-esteem [sometimes the Latin is translated as "self-satisfaction," sometimes "self-approval," and is understood by many as what they mean by "pride"] is a Joy born of the fact that a man considers himself and his own power of acting" (Definition XXV). He opposes such self-esteem to humility and tells us it "is really the highest thing we can hope for," so far as it arises from reason (*Ethics* IV, P52 Schol.). But that is not the point I wish to pursue here. I think we can now begin to see how an error of judgment can start looking like a sin in a God-centered world—at least when the error involves taking undeserved credit.

Spinoza picks up on Gregory the Great's vision of pride as bias in one's own favor, a tyranny of bad judgment: "it comes about that all the good things of others become displeasing to him, and the things he has done himself, even when they are mistaken, alone please him . . . he favours himself in his thought; and when he thinks he surpasses others in all things, he walks with himself along the broad spaces of his thought and silently utters his own praises" (*Moralia,* XXIV, 48, quoted in Payne 72–73). One might go further and think whatever praises are in fact due are due elsewhere, that when credit is traced to its ultimate source, pride in oneself is always misplaced.

## RESPONSIBILITY

One might think responsibility should be a condition of pride—that, for example, pride should be for virtue and achievements rather than natural endowment and gifts. Responsibility in turn might be seen as conditioned on causal role or individual choice. (The relevant conditions depend on the various purposes one might have in allocating responsibility; and for certain purposes, e.g., legal ones, getting the conditions precisely right might be extremely important [H. L. A. Hart].) But despite the many possible senses of "responsibility," responsibility is *not* a condition of pride. While there are conceptual constraints of other sorts on pride, there is no *conceptual* error in claiming to be proud where one cannot claim responsibility (whether one is proud of the 49ers, one's cultural heritage, one's parents, or one's height). If responsibility were a condition of pride, a politics of pride in group identity, where the characteristic defining group identity (whether skin color or sexual preference, ethnic or national origin) was not itself something deliberately chosen, would make no sense. The point of claiming such pride is different (and we shall return to it shortly), but it is worth lingering a moment longer on the temptation to condition pride on responsibility.

It might seem that, so far as group membership is dependent on factors outside of one's control, group membership cannot provide appropriate grounds for pride or, for that matter, for shame. One no more chooses one's family (or, more precisely, one's biological parents) than one chooses to be unattractive or unintelligent. Shame would seem as misplaced in the one case as in the others. But then, one typically does not become attractive or intelligent by one's choice and efforts; such advantages are typically gifts rather than achievements. So is pride appropriate in relation to such advantages? Certainly many are in fact proud of their looks or their intelligence. While such pride is not conceptually misplaced (responsibility is not, as a matter of language, a condition of pride), insofar as proper pride is thought to depend on achievements rather than gifts, it is perhaps morally misplaced. This may be part of the intuition of those who think of God as the author of our gifts, and so of individual pride in gifts as misappropriation of credit (if not sin). Leaving God aside, supposing one thinks proper pride must be limited to achievements rather than gifts (just as proper shame must be limited to faults rather than natural disadvantages or handicaps), the problem becomes most pointed when one asks whether perhaps *everything* isn't a gift? After all, traced far enough, even apparent achievements depend on conditions outside one's control.

The notion of "moral" appropriateness here connects with Kant's emphasis on the distinction between moral characteristics and natural characteristics. One's moral identity, for Kant, depends on factors outside the natural order. Appeal to the noumenal realm may take one beyond what empirically makes sense, but Kant's point connects with the ordinary intuition that there are some aspects of our character for which we are responsible (whether we try to work hard or are simply lazy, what we try to do with out intelligence, etc.) and there are others that are not subject to our will, but are simply (say biologically) given, and so not appropriate grounds for moral judgment. But then, will there not always be some empirical explanation for why some are lazy, why some try to do good with their intelligence, etc.? If one traces the causal chains far enough, won't we always come to factors outside the sphere of the individual will? One comes to doubt the line that depends on appeal to the individual (non-empirical) will. Kant's desire to isolate the sphere of the moral, marking it off as a sphere of freedom and autonomy, where moral—worth is a matter of virtue rather than natural endowment or talents viewed as gifts—may lead to a contracting self, a self with ultimately no content at all (Nagel). Certainly that is the result if everything ultimately is a gift. One writer, Arnold Isenberg (1949), sees the difficulty but tries to differentiate shame and pride, regarding pride as widely appropriate and shame as widely inappropriate, because he thinks shame does no good—it just adds misery to misery, and the reflexive misery is avoidable. But the pleasantness of an experience does not itself make that experience well grounded, and even misery can sometimes do some good (the spurrings of painful conscience may redirect just as bitter medicine may cure). Whatever the savings in individual misery, a society of the shameless is not highly to be desired.

While responsibility is not a condition of pride, something like "closeness to self" is. Seen as "close enough to ourselves," however that notion is unpacked, we can be proud or, equally, ashamed of our family or our country: they are a part of who one is and, even if one has not chosen them, one cannot wholly dissociate from them. That shame arguably should not extend to certain things outside our control—some things that are not our fault, such as physical limitations, handicaps, or deformities—is more a matter of what we regard as our "essential" self and what counts as valuable than of responsibility or control or the will (though some, like Kant, would shrink the essential self to a transcendent will). What should be regarded as essential and what as valuable are obviously contestable. That the chain of credit, "closeness to self" in Hume's phrase, is open to question in cases of group pride, such as that of the 49ers fans, opens the way to the insight that the chain of credit is in fact *always* open to question, even in cases of individual pride. The world in which individual pride was inevitably a sin took certain views of essential identity and of value as obvious. The politics of group pride seeks to question such views.

## VALUE

The political value of pride in identity politics partly derives from the internal place of values within pride. (When O. J. Simpson allowed as how he was "not proud" of his wife abuse, he was using "pride" to mark his choice of values, in this case to show his acceptance of community values.) On all accounts, the source of pride must be seen as an achievement or an advantage; pride involves position valuation. Like "closeness to self," that is a conceptual condition.

The point of pride as a member of a group, the pride of belonging, depends on some distinctive virtue of the group, on its perceived value. Claiming group membership is a way of claiming the associated value for oneself. This reflects the conceptual dependence of pride on positive valuation. (On Hume's excessively mechanical account, lacking the belief in value, one would lack the double association needed to produce pride. Rather, I would say, lacking the needed belief, whatever was produced would not be considered pride [cf. P. Foot].) That is, group pride, the pride of membership or belonging, like the pride of ownership, depends on value—the subject, like the owned object, is seen as valuable. The twist in recent identity politics is in the seeing of value.

Identity politics involves transvaluation, a reversal of received values: a previously despised property comes to be seen as valuable: "Black is Beautiful." Earlier majority values or norms are rejected as mistaken, biased, blind. A previous source of shame becomes a source of pride. The point is *not* that one should not be ashamed of one's skin color (for example) because one cannot help it, did not choose it, and so is not responsible. The point rather is that one should not be ashamed of one's skin color because there is nothing wrong with it in the first place.

One response is to see this as the politics of "sour grapes"—what "everyone knows" is valuable is rejected in self-defense against the shame of exclusion, of failure by the received standards. But if all that can be said in favor of a received standard is that "everyone knows" it is correct, that in itself provides grounds for suspicion. First there is the general bias in one's own favor that Spinoza warns of in connection with pride. The favored majority, the so-called "everyone," must beware of such self-reinforcing bias. Then there are more particular psychological tendencies to distortion, some especially prominent in recent local rivalries and nationalistic struggles. Issues of national identity are especially pressing in the many parts of the world where linguistic, religious, historical, and other divisions have taken on importance, sometimes leading to civil war. Such accentuation of small differences in the midst of overwhelming commonalities may be an inherent feature of human psychology, described by Freud under the heading of "the narcissism of minor differences." (The relation of such narcissism to identity formation and to aggression we will return to.) What differences are taken to matter and the value that is attached to the privileged position may very much depend on an individual's own situational circumstances and the accidents of history. Adjusting one's preferences to suit one's possibilities, making a virtue out of necessity (Elster 110), is as much a temptation for majorities as for minorities. Values are not to be reduced to uncriticized preferences. Better arguments more grounded in human nature and human needs must be provided if an accusation of "sour grapes" is to stick. And universal claims to dignity and justice weigh against it.

How is one to argue that one condition is better than another, that it ought to be preferred (even if it cannot be chosen, it is given or a "gift")? One should note first of all that such an argument does not by itself give grounds for preferential treatment. Indeed, preferential treatment, if any, might be better directed towards the socially disfavored condition. For example, it is plausible to suppose that it is almost always better to be intelligent than unintelligent (though during Red Guard purges of the intelligentsia and other such social upheavals, intelligence may come to have certain obvious disadvantages). But for educational purposes, it is arguable that a society that values equality should devote special resources to help the intellectually less gifted. What counts as a "special need" or, in the older terminology, a "handicap"? To say someone is "handicapped" is to say they are at a disadvantage. But disability is always relative to some purpose, and the value or disvalue of a disability must depend on the value, including the social usefulness, of the relevant power. Say one's powers of visual discrimination are limited, e.g., one is color blind. Or suppose one lacks a power of discrimination that only a few in fact possess (tea or wine tasters or perfume sniffers, persons of fine palate and olfactory discrimination): they can regularly note differences that those less empowered cannot, but are *most* of us thus handicapped? Is handicap necessarily a minority condition, so the norm is statistical? Is handicap necessarily a limitation of a socially important power, so lacking extraordinary powers is no handicap? Or is the value of a norm sometimes independent of how wide the distribution is and even of general social attitudes?

Thinking about deafness for a moment may help bring out the issues. The play (and movie) *Children of a Lesser God* makes an eloquent case for the beauty and power of signing as used by the deaf. Using sign language, one can even make points one cannot make or not make so forcefully as in, say, spoken English (the play illustrates this when "veal" on a menu is explained by poignantly combining the signs for "cow" and "baby"). While sign language is obviously different from oral speech, it nonetheless constitutes a fully structured language that can facilitate thought and interaction; and the insistence that deaf people leave it aside and learn to speak, an insistence that prevailed in institutions for the education of the deaf for a long period starting in the late nineteenth century, can be seen as a benighted prejudice (Sacks). It is nonetheless arguable that whatever the power and beauty of sign language as a language, whatever its intellectual and social usefulness, not hearing remains in any case a loss—and not just because the majority hear. In a majority deaf society, there might be a common language used by all (as in the Martha's Vineyard community discussed by Sacks [32–35]), and more accommodations might be made, but still most would be missing something, whether the warning noises of an approaching vehicle or the singing of birds. There are losses in not hearing, exclusions from aspects of life. In certain social conditions the losses might be less felt, but that does not make them any the less losses. (Though one must wonder whether if *no one* had the ability, it could still appear a loss. It would surely be odd for any human to experience the inability to fly as a "loss," as a handicap. But is that simply because it is odd for humans to compare themselves to birds rather than other humans?) None of this, again, is an argument against "Deaf Pride" as a political movement. That one might rather not be deaf is no reason to fail to respect the deaf, or to discriminate against them, or to fail to make accommodations. (Sacks writes: "The deaf do not regard themselves as handicapped, but as a linguistic and cultural minority" [138 n.147; 151].) Some disadvantages may be only socially imposed, and then the language of "handicap" or "special needs" may be inappropriate, but both socially imposed and natural disadvantages may often be ameliorated. In any case, the value claimed in all the movements that call for pride may ultimately be a matter of equal human dignity and respect and so may not turn on the difference between the chosen and the given or the socially useful and socially disfavored.

Another response is to think that rather than transvaluing an identity category, one ought to question the divisions and classifications themselves. Sometimes this is a matter of pointing out the predominance of gray. Sexual preferences and sexual activities allow for all degrees of exclusivity and combination. The exclusive heterosexual, in deed and fantasy, may be as rare as the exclusive homosexual. And even who counts as "black" is, despite what might appear a simple visual criterion, by no means always obvious. Lawrence Wright, in a *New Yorker* article entitled "One Drop of Blood," brings out how troubled the category is, in an interbreeding society, even for purposes of census taking (especially when tied to the distribution of social benefits). This is before issues of cultural and self-identification are introduced to complicate matters—whether a black child adopted and brought up by white parents in a white neighborhood is somehow thereby denied the blackness conferred by "black culture." An interracial society leads to multiracial individuals. But there are other problems with the socially constructed categories of individious discrimination than being sure who fits in them. The problem isn't just the existence of degrees of gray; some would reject the categories even in the supposedly clear cases.

Michel Foucault and some of his followers urge that a truly radical politics should emphasize resistance rather than liberation. Liberation, it is charged, involves accepting the categories of the powers that be, even when liberation insists on transvaluation (that is, asserting the positive value of the denigrated, marginalized category). Resistance, however, questions and rejects those categories. Thus David Halperin writes:

> The most radical reversal of homophobic discourses consists not in asserting, with the Gay Liberation Front of 1968, that "gay is good" (on the analogy with "black is beautiful") but in assuming and empowering a marginal positionality—not in rehabilitating an already demarcated, if devalued, identity but in taking advantage of the purely oppositional location homosexuality has been made to occupy. (61)

The rejection of categories in this sort of "queer" politics, a politics of positionality (of opposition, contrast, resistance) rather than identity, obscures (deliberately) the identity of the group being defended. That is, it objects to identity politics by attacking the terms of identity:

> To shift the position of "the homosexual" from that of object to subject is therefore to make available to lesbians and gay men a new kind of sexual identity, one characterized by its lack of a clear definitional content. The homosexual subject can now claim an identity without an essence. (61)

But the lack of a clear essence makes the alternative politics of positionality rather unclear. In Halperin's version, "queer" politics (vs. "gay" politics) includes all sexually marginalized individuals: "anyone who is or who feels marginalized because of her or his sexual practices: it could include some married couples without children, for example, or even (who knows?) some married couples *with* children." All that unites the group is its felt marginalization in relation to social norms—a definition that seems rather too broad for an organized group politics. (Put differently, the "subject position" emphasized is perhaps too subjective, however true it may be that we are *all* gay, all women, all black, for we are all marginalized, denigrated, despised, under some heading or other some of the time.) Halperin acknowledges (64) that the vast range of sexual outlaws (including sadomasochists, fetishists, pedarasts) can have diverse and divergent interests. There is another paradox here in a politics of positionality: aside from the fact that we are all somehow, in some aspect, outside the accepted norms, the supposed de-essentialized subject position requires that one feel marginalized in terms of a norm that is the norm of society or of "the others." Therefore, those norms and their understanding—objectification—reenter the picture: one's self-identity for oppositional purposes must depend on categories and norms provided from outside (at least if it is to count as "resistance" to those categories and norms), just as identity politics depends on those categories and norms before it undertakes its work of transvaluing them. Self-identification through desire may remain the best defense: "De-gaying gayness can only fortify homophobic oppression; it accomplishes in its own way the principal aim of homophobia: the elimination of gays. The consequence of self-erasure is . . . self-erasure. Even a provisional acceptance of the very categories elaborated by dominant identitarian regimes might more effectively undermine those forces than a simple disappearing act" (Bersani 5).

The appealing inclusiveness of "queer" rather than "lesbian and gay" politics becomes especially problematical when one considers the history of the extension and enforcement of rights as it has developed in the United States through legal protections for particular classifications of persons. How flexible can such legal categories be and where do they (must they) come from? Gays and lesbians have sought antidiscrimination laws and social recognition of our intimate associations. But no one that I know of has seriously proposed civil rights legislation ensuring nondiscrimination in employment and housing for sadomasochists (of course both homosexual and heterosexual). Why does that seem such an unpromising political agenda? (The notion of ensuring pedophiles the right to marry the boys they love raises further, special difficulties.) Must potential employers enquire about their employees' private sexual preferences in order to avoid unknowingly discriminating against them? (Is unknowing discrimination discrimination?) I will return to problems of "visibility" in a moment. Morris Kaplan, in a recent book on *Sexual Justice,* sensibly notes, "Adding 'lesbian' and 'gay' to 'heterosexual' in the repertoire of acceptable identities in our society would be a real but limited accomplishment in the struggle for full equality" (144). Anything short of equal treatment for all is rightly condemned as "limited," but civil rights for blacks were similarly "limited." The practices of discrimination however make some "limited" advances more pressing than others. (Are sadomasochists regularly discriminated against in employment and housing? Who would know?)

Whose oppression matters most? Here visibility plays a role, but it is multi-faced. The possibility of invisibility can provide protection that the law may deny. But the fact that one can hide one's sexual preferences, keep them private, is small consolation to those who regard those preferences as an important part of who they are, a part they do not wish to be obliged to conceal (especially given that there are advantages in being identifiable to those others who happen to share one's preferences). And of course, another side of the possibility of concealment, of passing, is the possibility of mistaken identification, of misidentification. Suppose someone was mistakenly identified as a member of a currently protected category (say of religion or race, say an Episcopalian was mistaken for a Catholic, or a very tan individual for an African American) by a potential employer or landlord and improperly discriminated against on the basis of that mistaken identification? Surely there is an intention to improperly discriminate. Would the victim have standing to sue under the statutes (given that he or she was not in fact a member of the protected category)? But then, in a world where sexual orientation was given specific protection, could anyone self-declare and then obtain legal redress? Transvestites are widely and mistakenly believed to all be homosexuals. Would a heterosexual transvestite mistakenly discriminated against as a homosexual have standing to sue under civil rights laws that protected gays but not transvestites? Again one feels the push towards the universal. Who decides who is in what category? It is worth noting that there is at the moment a movement afoot among some Orthodox Jewish Rabbis to denounce certain branches of Judaism, Conservative and Reform, as not-Jewish. Again, who decides? Is it the discriminators? The issue of attempted discrimination raises the question of whether the wrong is the mistake or the treating of *anyone* as though he or she was a second-class citizen, mistaken identification or correct notwithstanding. The question is whether antidiscrimination legislation can ultimately be understood as protecting individuals in certain categories, or all citizens. The rationale for such legislation turns on equal treatment for all, but the protections have had to be hard won in political contests, one despised category at a time.

Kaplan, like Halperin, may wish to protect all marginalized sexual outlaws, but in practice his argument has a narrower focus when he goes beyond those who would ask for no more than mere decriminalization of gay and lesbian sexual activity. Kaplan seeks specifically to add gays and lesbians to other protected categories (racial, religious, and ethnic groups, women, the physically and mentally handicapped, workers aged forty and older) for the purposes of protection against discrimination in employment, education, and housing. He argues:

> The underlying rationale of the anti-discrimination provisions of civil rights legislation is the recognition that formal legal equality is inadequate to provide for equal citizenship under conditions of popular hostility and pervasive social inequality. It is precisely the intensity and extent of the prejudice against homosexuality that justifies the claims of lesbian and gay citizens to protection against discrimination. (43)

And here he must have in mind extended histories of mistreatment, which have of course depended on identification by others, the mistreaters. Kaplan insists that "the definition of protected classes does not construct personal or political identities but rather forbids employers, landlords, and other decision makers from using such categories as race, religion, or sex to *impose* an invidious identity on a person rather than treating her in terms of her individual character and qualities" (45). He is certainly right about the point of such legislation. But if it is to be effectively enforced, it must specify the protected categories in a way that enables people to identify themselves under them for purposes of protection. And that risks the sort of rigidity and fixity that Kaplan wishes to avoid. I don't see how the law, for its purposes, which are indeed important, can avoid it. Moreover, the characteristics that are most significant, and so the ones most likely to be taken to be defining, are the very ones that decision makers (the discriminators and mistreaters) might be feared to improperly use—so perhaps it is the socially constructed categories, whatever the truth may be about essential characteristics, that become the most relevant ones. (As Hannah Arendt insisted: "If one is attacked as a Jew one must defend oneself as a Jew" [160].) Again, it is a history of popular hostility that makes something more than formal legal equality necessary.

Kaplan and Halperin are right to see the complexity, variety, and malleability of sexual desire. What follows for politics? Kaplan writes, "A politics based on fixed identities may foreclose the openness to contestation and negotiation required by justice" (112). That is surely a risk, but perhaps progress only gets made one step at a time. So far as Kaplan argues for antidiscrimination law, the groups to be protected must be defined in ways that make their members identifiable. A politics of legal reform must require the very "fixed identities" Kaplan seems to wish to deny. Of course they need not be fixed forever, or even for a lifetime, but they must be fixed for purposes of adjudication once one emerges from behind John Rawls's veil of ignorance into a world where some are identified (by others, if not themselves) as gay or lesbian and discriminated against on that basis.

It is difficult to see *what* one does differently when resisting a category rather than liberating or expressing an aspect of self seen under that category. And *who* one does it with is politically problematic. Is "queer" politics supposed to unite all who are non-mainstream sexually? The "we" here might include all sorts of folks who fit very uncomfortably with each other. Not that all gay folks are comfortable together. Our political views (like our sexual activities) cover as wide a spectrum as those of heterosexual folks. It is very difficult to see heterosexuals as a group with homogenized interests. The only reason it is easier for those who march under the banner of gay pride to be so seen is that they do have one important interest in common: sexual liberation and nondiscrimination on the basis of orientation; but they may not feel that way about all aspects of sexual expression ("sexual orientation"is doubtless the way the relevant category would be described for purposes of legislation, but what exactly would it cover?). Similarly, there are all sorts of political and social diversity among blacks, though all might agree that skin color is no proper ground for shame or discrimination. Political and social coalition among *all* racial and ethnic minorities has had a hard history, even if all might agree that skin color, place of origin, and cultural background are no proper grounds for shame or discrimination. It also might become unclear who the opposed "majority" is.

Of course there are problems with traditional identity politics, some stemming from the admitted grayness of categories. The problems of inclusion may be more serious than those raised by the 49er Faithful. What and who is *in* the category? Even a category such as race, which might appear straightforwardly biological, can be problematical; as noted, skin color may provide no sure index of anything and we may all in the end be multiracial. And again, gay behavior, desires and inclinations, and attitudes can all vary in more ways than marked even by Kinsey's categories (exclusive, occasional, etc.), and that before account is taken of the unconscious. Who are "we"? And if we think of the gay-identified as excluding the repressed or closeted homosexual, we may be focusing too much on the voluntaristic aspects of identification (like 49ers fans), where identification is self-identification. But where the political problem may arise from the identification, and stigmatization, by others, perhaps a politically relevant notion of identification must be broader (even if it risks objectification of individuals and reification of the categories of the others—after all, the struggle is with or against those very others). Even when one is not asked, and doesn't tell, one may be discriminated against, one's life restricted.

So far as the politics of marginal positionalities is aimed at denying privileged valuations of *either* side of dichotomies, the message may ultimately be the same as "Black is Beautiful" or "Gay is Good" or "Deaf Power." For the point, typically, is not to say black is better than white, or gay is better than straight, or deaf is better than hearing, but simply to deny the denigration of the minority position. The point is to demand political equality, equal concern and respect.

## THE NARCISSISM OF MINOR DIFFERENCES

Sigmund Freud observes that groups of individuals characteristically direct their greatest hostility towards those who, from a wider perspective, are in fact most similar to them. What is the source of this "narcissism of minor differences"? Is it an interesting but accidental sociological fact? Or is it somehow rooted in features of human psychology and the conditions for identity-formation; does it bespeak a natural polarity in thought?

Freud introduces the concept in his discussion of "The Taboo of Virginity" (1918). There the topic is male hostility to and fear of women and is complicated by the castration complex, but Freud is already prepared to make a point about individual separation and isolation ("that it is precisely the minor differences in people who are otherwise alike that form the basis of feelings of strangeness and hostility between them" [199]) and see in it "the hostility which in every human relation we see fighting successfully against feelings of fellowship and overpowering the commandment that all men should love one another" (199). When he turns to *Group Psychology* a few years later, he returns to the idea, there tying it to wider ambivalences as well as to narcissism (1921, 101). He develops the idea most fully in *Civilization and Its Discontents* where he discusses it in terms of aggression, which in this form serves "cohesion between the members of the community" against outsiders (1930, Ch. V, esp. 114). It is this final link, to what Freud regards as instinctual aggression, that may help clarify what may also be understood as a conceptual condition of identity formation. It makes conflict our normal state—and if pride is a sin, this (rather than intellectual error, even motivated intellectual error) may be its origin.

There is an old logical principle that holds "all determination is negation" *(Omnis determinatio est negatio),* and both individuals and communities often define themselves by opposition, by contrast, that is, in terms of what they reject. Stuart Hampshire elaborates the point in relation to incompatible conceptions of the good:

> Most influential conceptions of the good have defined themselves as rejections of their rivals: for instance, some of the ideals of monasticism were a rejection of the splendors and hierarchies of the Church, and this rejection was the original sense and purpose of the monastic ideal. Some forms of fundamentalism, both Christian and others, define themselves as a principled rejection of secular, liberal, and permissive moralities. Fundamentalism is the negation of any deviance in moral opinion, and of the very notion of opinion in ethics. (13)

People are who they are at least partly (and sometimes self-consciously) in terms of what they are not. The logical point is developed in Hegel and in F. H. Bradley. It is taken even further along a metaphysical dimension by Spinoza. As Hampshire puts Spinoza's vision: "Men and women are naturally driven to resist any external force that tends to repress their typical activities or to limit their freedom. . . . It is a natural necessity for each distinct entity to try to preserve its distinctiveness for as long as it can, and for this reason conflicts are at all times to be expected in the history of individuals, of social groups, and of nations, as their paths intersect" (Hampshire 15).

In psychoanalytical terms, the individual ego (and more specifically, the ego-ideal) is formed out of identifications and introjections, the other side of which is the rejection—typically a violent spitting out—of those characteristics one does not wish to incorporate: "At the very beginning, it seems, the external world, objects, and what is hated are identical. If later on an object turns out to be a source of pleasure, it is loved, but it is also incorporated into the ego" (Freud 1915, 136). As Norman O. Brown puts it, "The distinction between self and not-self is made by the childish decision to claim all that the ego likes as 'mine,' and to repudiate all that the ego dislikes as 'not-mine' " (142). The move from individual to group identity is explored in Freud's volume on *Group Psychology and the Analysis of the Ego* (1921), where his central concern is with groups, such as churches and armies, characterized by identification with a leader. The important role of unconscious mechanisms of identification via incorporation must complicate the too-simple voluntaristic picture of identity formation we started by considering in relation to the 49ers and other self-selecting groups of sports fans. As the existence of unconscious mechanisms should make clear, socially imposed identities are not the only alternative to consciously chosen identities. With unconscious mechanisms, ambivalence and aggression come to the fore. Others reject us, we reject others, and we project out "bad" and undesired aspects of ourselves while at the same time introjecting the desirable aspects of others.

Belonging to a group is tied to rejection of outsiders. Freud writes, "a religion, even if it calls itself the religion of love, must be hard and unloving to those who do not belong to it. Fundamentally indeed every religion is in this same way a religion of love for all those whom it embraces; while cruelty and intolerance towards those who do not belong to it are natural to every religion" (1921, 98). One might think that toleration and the embracing of diversity should provide a ready alternative, but history suggests vast impediments to such an alternative, and psychoanalysis sees aggression in the very mechanisms that serve to create a distinctive self or group. Freud's skepticism about demands to "love thy neighbour" and even "thine enemies" is tied to his belief in fundamental instincts of aggression (1930, ch. V). The sources of division and ambivalence run deep, perhaps deeper even than any putative aggressive instincts. All determination is negation. An embraced identity entails a rejected identity. Even the very languages that help define the identity of certain individuals and communities (not all Frenchmen need live in France) isolate and separate at the very time they unite (the story of Quebec is but one of many, very many, examples [see Ignatieff for more]). The ambiguity that some see in pride (arrogance vs. self-respect) may have behind it a deeper ambiguity in self-love and in identity itself (rejection and isolation vs. affirmation and community).

The ambiguities and ambivalences inevitably play themselves out in identity politics as well. Identity politics is by its nature divisive: it separates and distinguishes—though of course the distinctive categories are typically those provided by those who would discriminate against the minority, and the transvaluation of values is most often a form of (legitimate) self-defense. In narcissism, one rejects. In self-defense, one has been rejected. It is not enough to dismiss the imposed identities as false. New positive identities must be internalized and must be recognized. A universal identity and equality based on universal rights may be the ultimate aim, but the political question is how to get there from here. (And even a universal identity may have a price—one's distinctive ethnic, or religious, or sexual, or whatever identity may languish unacknowledged.)

When minorities engage in identity politics, asking for themselves what society should accord to all—dignity and respect and the equal protection of the laws—can they speak for all? When we gays and lesbians ask for antidiscrimination laws and social recognition of our intimate associations, who are "we"? Kaplan tells us Eve Kosofsky "Sedgwick marks a vacillation, within both homophobic and emancipatory discourses, between 'minoritizing' views of homosexuality that define a distinct group with a common identity and 'universalizing' views that link homosexuality to tendencies shared by all human beings" (160). That tension is pervasive. Again I ask, who are "we"? Perhaps like the non-Jewish Danish king who put on a Star of David when the Nazis decreed all Jews must wear the star, the better to single them out for persecution, we should all be Jews in a world of anti-Semitism. But how do we get to a world where we are all in this together, where no one is oppressed?

Who are "we" for purposes of political organization and activism, for purposes of demanding nondiscrimination, and so on? In a sense, of course, "we" is everyone, every citizen entitled to equal concern and respect and equal treatment under the law. But for purposes of the law, without denying or weakening the claims of anyone else, the adherents of gay pride can insist that experiencing same-sex desire or engaging in certain sexual practices with members of the same sex is no ground for invidious treatment, for discrimination in housing, education, or job opportunities. Perhaps one wants to say the same for other sexual minorities (and other nonsexual minorities as well). But so long as discrimination law singles out special categories for protection, one must be precise. There is not much to be gained by denying the reality of the very categories under which one is asking protection. If equal treatment for all is not enough to protect gays and lesbians, and we need to ask for specific protection, why should we be surprised if other sexual minorities need to do the same? Marginalized groups might wish to band together, but "queer" identity by itself may not do what is required.

## SELF-RESPECT AND SELF-ESTEEM

> The absence of sinful pride is called humility or modesty, but these apparent virtues hide their own faults and failings. Humility can give way to servility and obsequiousness—an exaggerated enhancement of the other's and a slavish devaluation of one's own worth. Modesty can lead to extremes of self-effacement, denials of one's existence and value that threaten social withdrawal or personal extinction. Poised somewhere between sinful vanity and self-destructive submissiveness is a golden mean of self-esteem appropriate to the human condition. Straying too far from it in either direction leads to active evil or passive victimization. (Lyman 135)

Aristotle's "proud" man is supposed to be a mean between the foolishly vain and the unduly humble (NE 1123b–1125a). (I am here following those translators who take *megalopsychia*—literally "greatness of soul"—to mean "pride." Others translate it as "magnanimity" and others still as "high-mindedness." It is the virtue "concerned with honour on the grand scale" and seems to essentially involve an ideal of pride and confident self-respect.) While the proud man's self-evaluation is supposed to be accurate (he "thinks himself worthy of great things, being worthy of them . . . he claims what is in accordance with his merits" [1123b]), and so his pride a virtue ("Pride, then, seems to be a sort of crown of the excellences" [1124a]), Aristotle's portrait of aristocratic disdain and self-sufficiency makes him sound like he suffers from what the later Christians regarded as the sin of pride. Aristotle's ideal great-spirited man has a lofty detachment from particular goods, save honor and dishonor. He cares most for honor, yet little even for that: "at honours that are great and conferred by good men he will be moderately pleased . . . for there can be no honour that is worthy of perfect excellence" (1124a); and tends to have detachment and disdain for the world in general ("honour from casual people and on trifling grounds he will utterly despise" [1124a] and "the proud man despises justly" [1124b] and "he is free of speech because he is contemptuous" [1124b]). He strives, all-in-all, for "a character that suffices to itself" (1125a).

Aristotle's proud man "is the sort of man to confer benefits, but he is ashamed of receiving them; for the one is the mark of a superior, the other of an inferior" (1124b). Even today, individuals who are described as "fiercely proud" are typically being singled out as especially independent. Some find it humiliating to be indebted, especially deeply indebted. Even a gift can humiliate. This can be understood broadly in terms of a general need to repay or reciprocate in human life: a whole theory of punishment flourishes under the heading of "retribution." Insults must be repaid, so must gifts—all are debts and create a burden. There are standards of reciprocity in human relations that can be felt as burdensome. (Some of the complexities here are nicely delineated by William Miller.) Of course, not accepting help (like, more obviously, not helping) can be a kind of aggression. The pride connected with independence and freedom from indebtedness can also be understood in terms of dependence (a central concern of Hegel) and power (a central concern of Nietzsche, who of course looked beyond virtue and sin). (See Neu 1996 on the unease of dependence.)

Some would distinguish between pride the sin and pride the emotion in terms of the former being a general character trait, though a person with the self-satisfied character trait might be especially liable to experience the corresponding emotion on a variety of occasions (as in Ryle's dispositional analysis of character traits such as vanity [85f]). As a matter of motivation, pride is expansive and goes with a tendency to display and show off (while shame is of course tied to a desire to hide, to disappear and become invisible). It is arguable that, even as a character trait, pride may not be a sin, or at least no longer a sin. Lyman suggests narcissism and pride are now a psychic necessity because of the need for individual strength in "the modern lonely age":

> The pattern of parental overestimation and excessive indulgence helps establish the psychic institution that must replace the now defunct social institutions of human conservation. Emancipation of the individual requires him to abandon his dependence on social security in favor of a hardly developed psychic self-sufficiency. The personal character appropriate to this liberating social structure is one in which pride must hold an important place. Less a sin than a necessity in the modern lonely age, pride is absolved from much of its guilt as the individual is freed from most of his constraints. (157)

The *sinful* character trait then might be equated to a kind of arrogance, as Schimmel puts it "exaggerating our worth and power, and feeling superior to others" (29). We are back to Spinoza's understanding of pride as bias in favor of oneself and excessive self-esteem. On the other hand, Gabrielle Taylor distinguishes the sin and the passion in terms of the sin involving a character trait where one's worth is taken for granted, and so one's high expectations may make particular occasions of pride the passion become relatively rare (1980 394ff; 1985 36ff). This may, like Aristotle, take the error out of the attitude. So, as sin, does the character trait necessarily involve error or not? Is a person with the character trait more or less likely to experience particular occasions of pride the emotion? Such occasions are based on particular reasons (one is "proud of this" or "because of that"). The generalized character trait of pride may need no reasons. But then "taking one's worth for granted" may be a matter of having a due regard for one's rights, may amount to self-respect. Self-respect also needs no reasons—in which case pride the character trait does *not* obviously amount to a sin, need not amount to presumptuous arrogance or anything more than self-assurance, or indeed, simple dignity.

There may be a contrast between self-esteem and self-respect that is helpful here. The pleasure that Hume discerns in pride is ultimately a form of self-approval (Neu 1977; Davidson 1980). But self-approval is ambiguous in a way that may help explain the dual attitudes, sin to be avoided and virtue to be sought, towards pride itself (whether regarded as a character trait or a passion). We can understand the ambiguity in terms of certain contrasts between self-esteem and self-respect. Self-respect, having to do with one's rights and dignity as a person, may be noncomparative. Self-esteem, having to do with one's merits and self-valuation, may depend on the standards of value in one's society and how one compares with other members of that society. Put crudely, of self-respect one cannot have too much; of self-esteem one obviously can. Put more precisely, the idea of too much self-respect is at best problematic, while that of too much self-esteem, like those of either too little self-respect or too little self-esteem, poses no difficulty. (See David Sachs [1981]). Cf. Rousseau's contrast of *amour de soi,* which is supposed to be natural, noncomparative, and tied to self-preservation, and *amour propre,* which is supposed to be social, comparative, and other-directed; see *Discourse on the Origin of Inequality* and *Emile,* Book IV.) Thus a person might have low self-esteem and yet have self-respect. As Sachs puts it, "it could be categorically true of a person both that he takes no pride in anything whatever, and yet that he has his pride" (350).

So far as pride is a matter of self-respect, one must have a certain amount. This point is developed by Thomas Hill (1973) who interprets certain forms of objectionable servility as resulting from misunderstanding one's moral rights or placing a comparatively low value on them, a lack of a certain type of self-respect, a respect that is owed one as a person, independently of special merits. That is, self-respect is a matter of appreciating one's equal moral rights as a person and (also perhaps) of living by one's own personal standards—not an issue of merits. Respect for one's merits, or esteem, is to be distinguished from respect for one's rights. Such a distinction helps clarify Edith Sitwell's attitude towards pride. While insisting it should not be confused with silly vanity or foolish obstinacy, Edith Sitwell declared: "Pride has always been one of my favourite virtues" (1962 15). She recognizes that pride "may be a form of love" (17), and she refers to "ugly humility" (19) and notes that "A proper pride is a necessity to an artist" (21). She sees it as a form of self-defense needed by the original against inevitable attacks by the envious and untalented. Such self-confidence needs to be understood in relation to self-respect (something essential to all) and self-esteem (which can be greater than justified, but also has a "proper" level). Everyone needs self-respect and is, moreover, entitled to it. It is a condition of moral identity.

One of the errors of certain recently popular self-help psychologies is to suppose that increasing self-esteem is simply a matter of changing one's attitude rather than the more strenuous activity of changing one's life. So far as esteem depends on merit, a pride that simply depends on deciding one is "ok" whatever one does becomes like the sinful individual pride of old: one falls into unjustifiable self-satisfaction. Group credit too, or "bragging rights," does little to advance claims based on merit unless responsibility (as well as "nearness") can somehow be claimed. So far as the group pride gives self-respect and asks for respect from others based on one's common humanity and equal moral rights, there is no sin, no error. But one should be careful of too simply tying the contrast between pride as sin and as virtue to the contrast of self-esteem and self-respect, for while self-esteem can be excessive (a person can think too well of themselves), there is surely a "correct" or justified level of self-esteem, which might be quite high in some cases (even if not quite so high as in the case of Aristotle's great-souled man).

We have seen that nearness to self is necessary to distinguish pride from mere happiness or joy; that is, pride is self-enhancing. Taking credit for a valuable object expands our identity, enhances our self-esteem. So one can see how pride can be competitive, concerned as it is with ego-identity and its enhancement, and it is thus subject to envy and liable to fall into sinful arrogance. Arrogance may be the heart of (certain understandings of) pride the sin. It is the antithesis of the concern for equality in self-respect. It is the excessive self-esteem emphasized by Spinoza, a bias in favor of oneself that may seem more a general character trait than a particular emotion. If self-esteem is understood as based on perceived merits, then it is perhaps more like pride the emotion which is also based on particular reasons. Enough such pride amounts to conceit, the character trait of thinking too well of oneself (even if one has particular reasons). But self-respect needs no reasons and so is more like a generalized pride that is more like a character trait—but, again, it is then *not* obviously a sin, need not amount to presumptuous arrogance or anything more than self-assurance or dignity.

The cardinal (or chief) sins were in the beginning not necessarily mortal (or deadly) ones. Their importance attached to those temptations with special significance from a monastic point of view—that of Evagrius of Pontus and John Cassian, the fathers of the seven cardinal sins in the fourth and fifth centuries. There is the familiar phenomenon of pride in one's humility. Cassian points out that "Pride is the most savage of all evil beasts, and the most dreadful, because it lies in wait for those who are perfect" (quoted in Payne 68). The early lists sometimes had eight sins—sometimes, for example, distinguishing *vana gloria* (vainglory) from *superbia* (pride). The lists later came to serve penitential purposes with priests using them as a helpful aid in the examination of conscience for confession, and the distinction previously made between cardinal and deadly sins dropped away. As St. Thomas pointed out, a sin is called capital "simply because other sins frequently arise from it" (*DeMalo* IX.2-5, quoted in Bloomfield 88).

Pride's special importance among even the deadly sins Aquinas attributed to its general character which made it arguably the source of all sins insofar as it involves a turning-away from God [. . . . Aquinas 314ff.) The specific sins each in their own way involve rebellion against the law of God, but such rebellion is the essence of pride as a general sin. In its more specific form, vainglory, it involves an inordinate desire for honor and renown, a special admiration of one's own excellences. And it was of course vanity rather than pride that became the focus of (the relatively godless) later French moralists. Vanity is especially concerned with public reputation. Pride is the sin of not knowing one's place and sticking to it. It is of course Faust's ambitious sin. Challenging God—going above your place.

Greek hubris (thinking oneself superior to the gods), like Christian pride (thinking oneself independent of God, self-sufficient), involves placing oneself above one's station. This is one of the features of pride that makes it peculiarly appropriate as the banner for political movements that seek to change the station of those in them—i.e., that seek a transvaluation of values. Both identity politics and a politics of marginal positionalities, whatever their views on whether God has died, deny that the social valuations and positions that denigrate certain groups and privilege others are ordained by God. Times have changed. The death of God would leave the concept of sin with little conceptual foothold. But even in a world where God is still believed to preside, an attack on social hierarchy need not be regarded as sin, for it is not an attack on God: social hierarchy is not a matter of natural law, is not God-given. These political movements are challenging positions in the political world rather than a God-given order. And, as we have seen, on an individual level, the self-approval that is characteristic of pride may be ambiguous, and the different significances may be understood in terms of a contrast between self-esteem (which can be excessive and unjustified) and self-respect (which does not depend on invidious comparison and may be essential to human dignity). A politics of self-respect, where the self has a social identity, may not be so ungodly after all.

## REFERENCES

Aquinas, St. Thomas (1995 [1269]). *On Evil*, trans. Jean Oesterle. Notre Dame, Ind.: University of Notre Dame Press.

Aristotle (1984). *Nicomachean Ethics*, in *The Complete Works of Aristotle*, Vol. II, ed. Jonathan Barnes. Princeton: Princeton University Press.

Bersani, Leo (1995). *Homos*. Cambridge: Harvard University Press.

Bloomfield, Morton W. (1952). *The Seven Deadly Sins: An Introduction to the History of a Religious Concept, with Special Reference to Medieval English Literature*. East Lansing: Michigan State College Press.

Brown, Norman O. (1966). *Love's Body*. New York: Vintage Books.

Davidson, Donald (1980 [1976]). Hume's Cognitive Theory of Pride. In *Essays on Actions and Events* (pp. 277–90). New York: Oxford University Press.

Elster, Jon (1983). Sour Grapes. In *Sour Grapes: Studies in the Subversion of Rationality* (pp. 109–140). Cambridge: Cambridge University Press.

Fairlie, Henry (1979). Pride or Superbia. In *The Seven Deadly Sins Today* (pp. 39–58). Notre Dame, Ind.: University of Notre Dame Press.

Foot, Philippa (1978 [1958–59]). Moral Beliefs. In *Virtues and Vices* (pp. 110–31). Berkeley: University of California Press.

Freud, Sigmund (1915). Instincts and their Vicissitudes. *Standard Edition* Vol. XIV. London: Hogarth Press.

Freud, Sigmund (1918 [1917]). The Taboo of Virginity. *Standard Edition* Vol. XI. London: Hogarth Press.

Freud, Sigmund (1921). *Group Psychology and the Analysis of the Ego*. *Standard Edition* Vol. XVIII. London: Hogarth Press.

Freud, Sigmund (1930 [1929]). *Civilization and Its Discontents*. *Standard Edition* Vol. XXI. London: Hogarth Press.

Halperin, David M. (1995). *Saint Foucault: Towards a Gay Hagiography*. New York: Oxford University Press.

Hampshire, Stuart (1996). Justice is Conflict: The Soul and the City. Tanner Lectures on Human Values, Harvard University, October 30–31, 1996. [unpublished ms]

Hart, H. L. A. (1968). Responsibility. In *Punishment and Responsibility: Essays in the Philosophy of Law* (pp. 211–30). New York: Oxford University Press.

Hill, Thomas E., Jr. (1991 [1973]). Servility and Self-Respect. in *Autonomy and Self-Respect* (pp. 4–18). Cambridge: Cambridge University Press.

Hume, David (1888 [1739]). *A Treatise of Human Nature* [THN], ed. L. A. Selby-Bigge. New York: Oxford University Press.

Ignatieff, Michael (1993). *Blood and Belonging: Journeys into the New Nationalism.* New York: Farrar, Straus & Giroux.

Isenberg, Arnold (1980 [1949]). Natural Pride and Natural Shame. In A. Rorty, ed., *Explaining Emotions* (pp. 355–83). Berkeley: University of California Press.

Kant, Immanuel (1964 [1797]). *The Metaphysical Principles of Virtue,* trans. J. Ellington. Indianapolis: Bobbs-Merrill.

Kaplan, Morris (1997). *Sexual Justice: Democratic Citizenship and the Politics of Desire.* New York: Routledge.

Lyman, Stanford M. (1978). *The Seven Deadly Sins: Society and Evil.* New York: St. Martin's Press.

Miller, William Ian. (1993). *Humiliation.* Ithaca: Cornell University Press.

Nagel, Thomas (1979 [1976]). Moral Luck. In his *Mortal Questions* (pp. 24–38). Cambridge: Cambridge University Press.

Neu, Jerome (1977). *Emotion, Thought, and Therapy.* London: Routledge & Kegan Paul and University of California Press.

Neu, Jerome (1996). *Odi et Amo:* On Hating the Ones We Love. In J. O'Neill, ed., *Freud and the Passions* (pp. 53–72). University Park: Pennsylvania State University Press.

Payne, Robert (1960). *Hubris: A Study of Pride.* New York: Harper Torchbooks.

Ryle, Gilbert (1949). *The Concept of Mind.* London: Hutchinson.

Sachs, David (1981). How to Distinguish Self-Respect from Self-Esteem. *Philosophy and Public Affairs,* 10, 346–60.

Sacks, Oliver (1990. *Seeing Voices: A Journey into the World of the Deaf.* New York: HarperPerennial.

Schimmel, Solomon (1992). *The Seven Deadly Sins: Jewish, Christian, and Classical Reflections on Human Nature.* New York: Free Press.

Sitwell, Edith (1962). Pride. In Angus Wilson et al., *The Seven Deadly Sins* (pp. 15–22). New York: William Morrow & Co.

Smith, Adam (1969 [1759]). *The Theory of Moral Sentiments.* Indianapolis: Liberty Classics.

Spinoza (1985 [1677]). *Ethics,* in *The Collected Works of Spinoza,* Vol. I, ed. and trans. Edwin Curley. Princeton: Princeton University Press.

Taylor, Charles (1992). *The Ethics of Authenticity.* Cambridge: Harvard University Press.

Taylor, Gabriele (1980) Pride. In A. Rorty, ed., *Explaining Emotions* (pp. 385–402). Berkeley: University of California Press.

Taylor, Gabriele (1985). *Pride, Shame, and Guilt.* New York: Oxford University Press.

Walsh, W. H. (1970). Pride, Shame and Responsibility. *The Philosophical Quarterly,* 20, 1–13.

Wright, Lawrence (1994). One Drop of Blood. *The New Yorker,* 70 (July 25, 1994), 46ff.

# 3

## SLOTH

### Thomas Pynchon

In his classical discussion of the subject in the *Summa Theologica*, Aquinas termed Sloth, or *acedia*, one of the seven capital sins. He said he was using "capital" to mean "primary" or "at the head of" because such sins gave rise to others, but there was an additional and darker sense resonating luridly just beneath and not hurting the power of his argument, for the word also meant "deserving of capital punishment." Hence the equivalent term "mortal," as well as the punchier English "deadly."

But come on, isn't that kind of extreme—death for something as lightweight as Sloth? Sitting there on some medieval death row, going, "So, look, no offense, but what'd they pop you for anyway?"

"Ah, usual story, they came around at the wrong time of day, I end up taking out half of some sheriff's unit with my two-cubit crossbow, firing three-quarter-inch bolts on auto feed. Anger, I guess. . . . How about you?"

"Um, well . . . it wasn't anger. . . ."

"Ha! Another one of these Sloth cases, right?"

". . . fact, it wasn't even me."

"Never is, slugger—say, look, it's almost time for lunch. You wouldn't happen to be a writer, by any chance?"

Writers of course are considered the mavens of Sloth. They are approached all the time on the subject, not only for free advice, but also to speak at Sloth Symposia, head up Sloth Task Forces, testify as expert witnesses at Sloth Hearings. The stereotype arises in part from our conspicuous presence in jobs where pay is by the word and deadlines are tight and final—we are presumed to know from piecework and the convertibility of time and money. In addition, there is all the glamorous folklore surrounding writer's block, an affliction known sometimes to resolve itself dramatically and without warning, much like constipation, and (hence?) finding wide sympathy among readers.

Writer's block, however, is a trip to the theme park of your choice alongside the mortal sin that produces it. Like each of the other six, Sloth was supposed to be the progenitor of a whole family of lesser, or venial sins, among them Idleness, Drowsiness, Restlessness of the Body, Instability, and Loquacity. *Acedia* in Latin means sorrow, deliberately self-directed, turned away from God, a loss of spiritual determination that then feeds back on in to the process, soon enough producing what are currently known as guilt and depression, eventually pushing us to where we will do anything, in the way of venial sin and bad judgment, to avoid the discomfort.

But Sloth's offspring, though bad—to paraphrase the Shangri-Las—are not always evil, for example what Aquinas terms Uneasiness of the Mind, or "rushing after various things without rhyme or reason," which "if it pertains to the imaginative power . . . is called curiosity." It is of course precisely in such episodes of mental traveling that writers are known to do good work, sometimes even their best, solving formal problems, getting advice from Beyond, having hypnagogic adventures that with luck can be recovered later on. Idle dreaming is often of the essence of what we do. We sell our dreams. So real money actually proceeds from Sloth, although this transformation is said to be even more amazing elsewhere in the entertainment sector, where idle exercises in poolside loquacity have not infrequently generated tens of millions of dollars in revenue.

As a topic for fiction, Sloth over the next few centuries after Aquinas had a few big successes, notably Hamlet, but not until arriving on the shores of America did it take the next important step in its evolution. Between Franklin's hectic aphorist, Poor Richard, and Melville's doomed scrivener, Bartleby, lies about a century of early America, consolidating itself as a Christian capitalist state, even as *acedia* was in the last stages of its shift over from a spiritual to a secular condition.

Philadelphia, by Franklin's time, answered less and less to the religious vision that William Penn had started off with. The city was becoming a kind of high-output machine, materials and labor going in, goods and services coming out, traffic inside flowing briskly about a grid of regular city blocks. The urban mazework of London, leading into ambiguities and indeed evils, was here all rectified, orthogonal. (Dickens, visiting in 1842, remarked, "After walking about in it for an hour or two, I felt that I would have given the world for a crooked street.") Spiritual matters were not quite as immediate as material ones, like productivity. Sloth was no longer so much a sin against God or spiritual good as against a particular sort of time, uniform, one-way, in general not reversible—that is, against clock time, which got everybody early to bed and early to rise.

Poor Richard was not shy in expressing his distaste for Sloth. When he was not merely repeating well-known British proverbs on the subject, he was contributing Great Awakening-style outbursts of his own— "O Lazy-bones! Dost think God would have given thee arms and legs if he had not designed thou shouldst use them?" Beneath the rubato of the day abided a stern pulse beating on, ineluctable, unforgiving, whereby whatever was evaded or put off now had to be made up for later, and at a higher level of intensity. "You may delay, but time will not." And Sloth, being continual evasion, just kept piling up like a budget deficit, while the dimensions of the inevitable payback grew ever less merciful.

In the idea of time that had begun to rule city life in Poor Richard's day, where every second was of equal length and irrevocable, not much in the course of its flow could have been called nonlinear, unless you counted the ungovernable warp of dreams, for which Poor Richard had scant use. In Frances M. Barbour's 1974 concordance of the sayings, there is nothing to be found under "Dreams," dreams being as unwelcome in Philly back then as their frequent companion, sleep, which was considered time away from accumulating wealth, time that had to be tithed back into the order of things to purchase twenty hours of productive waking. During the Poor Richard years, Franklin, according to the *Autobiography*, was allowing himself from 1 A.M. to 5 A.M. for sleep. The other major nonwork block of time was four hours, 9 P.M. to 1 A.M., devoted to the Evening Question, "What good have I done this day?" This must have been the schedule's only occasion for drifting into reverie—there would seem to have been no other room for speculations, dreams, fantasies, fiction. Life in that orthogonal machine was supposed to be nonfiction.

By the time of *Bartleby the Scrivener: A Story of Wall Street* (1853), *acedia* had lost the last of its religious reverberations and was now an offense against the economy. Right in the heart of robber-baron capitalism, the title character develops what proves to be terminal *acedia*. It is like one of those Western tales where the desperado keeps making choices that only herd him closer to the one disagreeable finale. Bartleby just sits there in an office on Wall Street repeating, "I would prefer not to." While his options go rapidly narrowing, his employer, a man of affairs and substance, is actually brought to question the assumptions of his own life by this miserable scrivener—this writer!—who, though among the lowest of the low in the bilges of capitalism, nevertheless refuses to go on interacting anymore with the daily order, thus bringing up the interesting question: who is more guilty of Sloth, a person who collaborates with the root of all evil, accepting things-as-they-are in return for a paycheck and a hassle-free life, or one who does nothing, finally, but persist in sorrow? *Bartleby* is the first great epic of modern Sloth, presently to be followed by work from the likes of Kafka, Hemingway, Proust, Sartre, Musil, and others—take your own favorite list of writers after Melville and you're bound sooner or later to run into a character bearing a sorrow recognizable as peculiarly of our own time.

In this century we have come to think of Sloth as primarily political, a failure of public will allowing the introduction of evil policies and the rise of evil regimes, the worldwide fascist ascendancy of the 1920s and 1930s being perhaps Sloth's finest hour, though the Vietnam era and the Reagan–Bush years are not far behind. Fiction and nonfiction alike are full of characters who fail to do what they should because of the effort involved. How can we not recognize our world? Occasions for choosing good present themselves in public and private for us every day, and we pass them by. *Acedia* is the vernacular of everyday moral life. Though it has never lost its deepest notes of mortal anxiety, it never gets as painful as outright despair, or as real, for it is despair bought at a discount price, a deliberate turning against faith in anything because of the inconvenience faith presents to the pursuit of quotidian lusts, angers, and the rest. The compulsive pessimist's last defense (stay still enough and the blade of the scythe, somehow, will pass by), Sloth is our background radiation, our easy-listening station—it is everywhere, and no longer noticed.

Any discussion of Sloth in the present day is of course incomplete without considering television, with its gifts of paralysis, along with its creature and symbiont, the notorious Couch Potato. Tales spun in idleness find us tubeside, supine, chiropractic fodder, sucking it all in, reenacting in reverse the transaction between dream and revenue that brought these colored shadows here to begin with so that we might feed, uncritically, committing the six other deadly sins in parallel: eating too much, envying the celebrated, coveting merchandise, lusting after images, angry at the news, perversely proud of whatever distance we may enjoy between our couches and what appears on the screen.

Sad but true. Yet, chiefly owing to the timely invention—not a minute too soon!—of the remote control and the VCR, maybe there is hope after all. Television time is no longer the linear and uniform commodity it once was. Not when you have instant channel selection, fast-forward, rewind, and so forth. Video time can be reshaped at will. What may have seemed under the old dispensation like time wasted and unrecoverable is now perhaps not quite as simply structured. If Sloth can be defined as the pretense, in the tradition of American settlement and spoliation, that time is one more nonfinite resource, there to be exploited forever, then we may for now at least have found the illusion, the effect, of controlling, reversing, slowing, speeding, and repeating time—even imagining that we can escape it. Sins against video time will have to be radically redefined.

Is some kind of change already in the offing? A recent issue of the *National Enquirer* announced the winner of their contest for the King of Spuds, or top Couch Potato in the United States, culled from about a thousand entries.

> "All I do is watch television and work," admits the 35-year-old bachelor, who keeps three TV sets blaring 24 hours a day at his Fridley, Minn., home and watches a fourth set on the job.
> "There's nothing I like more than sitting around with a six-pack of beer, some chips and a remote control. . . . The TV station even featured me in a town parade. They went into my house, got my couch and put it on a float. I sat on the couch in my bathrobe and rode in the parade!"

Sure, but is it Sloth? The fourth television set at work, the fact that twice, the Tuber in question mentions sitting and not reclining, suggest something different here. Channel-surfing and VCR-jockeying may require a more nonlinear awareness than may be entirely compatible with the venerable sin of Sloth—some inner alertness or tension, as of someone sitting in a yoga posture, or in Zen meditation. Is Sloth once more about to be, somehow, transcended? Another possibility of course is that we have not passed beyond *acedia* at all, but that it has only retreated from its long-familiar venue, television, and is seeking other, more shadowy environments—who knows? computer games, cult religions, obscure trading floors in faraway cities—ready to pop up again in some new form to offer us cosmic despair on the cheap.

Unless the state of our souls becomes once more a subject of serious concern, there is little question that Sloth will continue to evolve away from its origins in the long-ago age of faith and miracle, when daily life really was the Holy Ghost visibly at work and time was a story, with a beginning, middle, and end. Belief was intense, engagement deep and fatal. The Christian God was near. Felt. Sloth—defiant sorrow in the face of God's good intentions—was a deadly sin.

Perhaps the future of Sloth will lie in sinning against what now seems increasingly to define us—technology. Persisting in Luddite sorrow, despite technology's good intentions, there we'll sit with our heads in virtual reality, glumly refusing to be absorbed in its idle, disposable fantasies, even those about superheroes of Sloth back in Sloth's good old days, full of leisurely but lethal misadventures with the ruthless villains of the Acedia Squad.

# 4

# GREED

## James Ogilvy

G reed is first among the seven deadlies. Greed turns love into lust, leisure into sloth, hunger into gluttony, honor into pride, righteous indignation into anger, and admiration into envy. If it weren't for greed, we'd suffer fewer of the other vices.

So seen as the premier sin, greed is to the vices what justice is to the virtues. Plato's dialogues demonstrate the unity of the virtues, with justice playing the role of first among equals. You can't have just one virtue without having them all, especially justice. Courage, for example, becomes foolish bravado without the moderating influence of temperance. Justice is the final moderator, the principle of balance that keeps each of the virtues from turning over into its opposite, an immoderate vice. Greed is precisely the opposite of justice. Greed is outstandingly immoderate. As such, it destroys balance, drives us to extremes, and serves as the very engine of vice. Should we therefore launch our moral rearmament by rooting out greed? I'll argue not, for the following reasons.

Greed is best understood as desire run amok. But desire, I'll argue, is a good thing, not the bad thing that ascetics would have us spurn. One's very identity gets defined by the desires one gratifies. And intense desires help to define the kinds of selves we would like to be: not bland, but vivid; not desireless, but avid . . . if not avaricious. But here's the rub: while intense desires may carve a more vivid identity than bland indifference, desire that crosses over into greed becomes self-defeating.

Greed construed as too much of a good thing is far more pernicious than greed construed as an unqualified bad thing. Temptations to greed are dangerous to our mental health because they mimic the strong desires that make us who we are. And temptations to greed are growing these days. Just as Oscar Wilde quipped that he could resist anything but temptation, so many of us become deluded by our desires into desiring greed.

Many people are now suffering under the delusion that just because communism proved to be a dead end, the unbridled greed of the rampant capitalist must be okay. No. This binary framework is misleading. Just because anorexia is (literally) a psychosomatic dead end, it does not follow that obesity is a good thing.

Granting that obesity is unhealthy, however, does it follow that each of us should strive to be as thin as possible, short of anorexia? Obesity is not so bad that we should cease indulging in an occasional dessert. Likewise, just because communism is a dead end, it does not follow that the accumulation of limitless wealth is a good thing. Nor does it follow that we should limit our possessions to a minimum of basic needs.

In this essay I seek a middle ground between asceticism and the greedy pursuit of obscene wealth. My thesis amounts to a defense of consumerism against three different sets of critics: first, against ascetics who want to purge the soul of all desires and their satisfactions; second, against those who fail to see the benefits of private property; and third, against overzealous capitalists who fail to see when a good thing— private property—becomes too much of a good thing.

I will call this middle ground between asceticism and greed the domain of *proper property:* not no property, as suffered under voluntary asceticism or involuntary poverty; not too much property, as pursued by greed; but proper property—at least enough to satisfy most needs and in many cases enough to define a lifestyle and an identity, but not so much as to do harm to oneself or others.

Finding this middle ground is harder than it looks. I'll take some time to dismiss some attempts that I regard as misleading or simply false. For example, I'll try to show that at the lower end of proper property, the "poverty line" is bound to be a moving target that can't be drawn once and for all by a permanent boundary separating true needs from false needs. Further, at the upper end of proper property, it's equally difficult to determine once and for all where property turns from proper to obscene. It's hard to know when a good thing becomes too much of a good thing.

Crossing this latter line is, I believe, what worries us most about greed. Apart from Gordon Gekko's radical defense in the movie *Wall Street*—his far too simple statement that "Greed is good!"—most of us believe that greed, along with the other six deadly sins, is an evil to be avoided like the plague. Though I cannot speak for the authors of other essays in his book, I suspect that at least some of them share some version of a contrary belief: namely, that virtues are not as separable from vices as sheep from goats; that the attempt to so separate them is dangerously naive; and that real virtue demands a certain familiarity with the vices and an acknowledgment of their inescapability. So rather than falling into the vice of a holier-than-thou pride, rather than imagining that one can avoid vice altogether, it would be better to gain some familiarity with the vices and, along with that familiarity, the ability to live virtuously *with* them rather than (allegedly, but impossibly innocently) entirely without them.

In seeking greater familiarity with greed, I want to find a more nuanced appreciation than one finds in Adam Smith or Milton Friedman. Rather than simply attacking greed or defending greed, I want to offer an account that shows the good reasons we have for flirting with temptations toward what I'll acknowledge to be evil consequences. I will assume as background for my argument an open future that is not predetermined. As a consequence of that open future, I assume a certain amount of human freedom. I am not claiming nor will I argue for a heroic subject who is autonomous—only that we lack a satisfactory owner's manual for the human spirit. There may be a science for maximizing the yield on asparagus, but there is no science for growing the best humans. Because the human condition includes a mental capacity for manipulating symbols into ever new meanings, and we retain a modicum of freedom to choose the meanings that motivate us most deeply, it will never be possible to predetermine once and for all the best rules for playing the human game. In order to make good on our freedom, in order to keep testing the limits of what our histories and cultures have given us to play with, human beings will continue to push out the boundaries of acceptable behavior.

I'm claiming this abiding temptation to transgression as an ambient background for all of the vices, not just greed. But I'll restrict most of my attention to the way this temptation plays out in the particular case of greed. It's not enough to accept desire and then imagine that you can draw a clear and easy line between desire as good and greed as bad and avoidable. No, once you admit the goodness of desire (a case that remains to be made against ascetics), then it becomes extremely difficult to avoid the temptations of greed. Not impossible. I will *not* argue that desire is good, that greed is indistinguishable from strong desire, and therefore that greed is good. My argument is subtler than that. Roughly, and unsubtly, I will argue that desire is good, and greed so difficult to distinguish from intense desire that attempts to avoid all greed run the risk of suppressing desire, and that is bad, and that is why we *should not* try to permanently avoid the temptations of greed. This is different, subtly but importantly different, from saying that we *should* indulge in greed.

The key to the argument I will make lies in the distinction between need and desire. Needs are imperious. You *have to have* water or you die. Desires, on the other hand, are optional. Granting that we'll need to pay much more attention to a gray area where strong desire takes on the psychological exigency of need ("I'll just die if I don't get that house!"), the point I want to stress here is this: as opposed to the imperious nature of need, the optional nature of desire opens up the arena to the influence of mind. Bodies have needs; people with minds have desires. The point I want to press just now is the good news/bad news implications of claiming mind as the differentiator of desire from need.

The good news unfolds in the form of a defense of consumerism: showing how the gratification of desire through the acquisition of possessions in the marketplace does much more than merely satisfy biological needs. Consumption (not just production) can serve as a medium for the creation and expression of character and individuality. Contrary to a tradition that privileges the activity of production and the value of productivity over the apparent passivity of mere consumption, I'll argue that consumption is a legitimate arena for human self-realization.

The bad news implicit in the role of mind in desire (as distinct from the mindlessness of need) is the potential for desire run amok turning into greed. Where needs yield to finite and unambiguous satisfactions—a full stomach, a quenched thirst—desires, precisely to the extent that they are fed by mind, can reel off into an infinite longing that can never be satisfied. Precisely to the extent that mind can always imagine some further variation on the object of desire, some further comparison with someone else's property, some further form of satisfaction—desire, strong desire, is ever susceptible to broaching over into the vice of greed. By approaching greed as too much of a good thing I am not offering an unqualified defense of greed; but I am showing how and why its temptation is unavoidable for active minds trying to get the most out of life.

I am saying that desire is a good thing, that the embellishment of need by mind renders animal requirements into genuinely human delights; further, I will argue that, up to a point, more desire is better than less desire. This last point, the defense of intense desire, has to be limited in its scope. This is not an argument about "human nature," or about all people at all times in all places. My argument does not extend its scope to cover Muslims, Hindus, or Aborigines, but it does say something about the heirs of modern European history who are now engaged in a transition from an industrial economy to an information/services economy. Whatever role intense desire may have played in Adam Smith's day, I want to claim that its role today is heightened by the degree to which advanced economies are shifting from the satisfaction of universal needs to the gratification of particular wants and desires. This shift changes the balance between the need for heightened production to satisfy needs and heightened consumption to gratify desires.

Surprising as it may seem to macroeconomists who see productivity as the primary driver of national economies, I want to show how intense desire is playing an ever greater role in maintaining a healthy economy. The marketplace, I will argue, is the best means of gratifying particular desires, however good central planning may be at satisfying universal needs. I will offer a defense of market mechanisms that is the opposite of the old "trickle down" argument. I will show how the trickling up of consumer preferences based on their particular desires does a better job of matching supply and demand than either central planning or the trickling down of excess wealth produced by rampant greed.

So that is the overall strategy of this essay: to show, first, why desire is preferable to desirelessness; second, how some greed is almost inevitable once desire has been accepted; and third, how to manage the intrinsically messy line between desire and greed in order to avoid aspiring to too much of a good thing.

Consider an example to capture the trajectory of the following argument: the technologies of travel and speed. Ivan Illich makes a fairly persuasive argument that the speed of a bicycle is the optimum top speed of human locomotion. By calculating the overall time a society devotes to travel and the production of the means of travel, Illich argues that once we arrange our society in such a way that many of us need to commute by car, then we end up spending more time and energy, not less, on creating and using our technologies of locomotion.[1] Should we then restrict ourselves to bicycles? Should we speak of "true needs" for bicycles and call the need for cars, trains, and airplanes "false needs"? I will argue that it is not possible to fix a single velocity at which the desire for speed turns from "true" to "false" and, further, that when you want to get somewhere in a hurry, more speed is usually better than less speed, so a stronger desire for speed will be preferable to a weaker one although, finally, there is a danger of indulging in too much of a good thing. Beware reckless driving, and drive fuel efficient, clean-burning vehicles. But note how these final cautions have as much to do with the manner of consumption—how you drive and what you drive—as with production: the availability of high mileage vehicles. By shifting attention from the supply side to the demand side of the commercial equation, I want to show how intense desire, bordering on greed, can shape the evolution of consumer goods toward higher quality and, in the process, shape consumers into more discriminating, more highly developed human beings.

## TRANSCENDING DESIRELESSNESS

You don't have to be a Buddhist to hear the call of asceticism. It cries out from the depths of the Western tradition from Plato and St. Augustine through René Descartes and Karl Marx. Without assuming any familiarity with the original texts, I want to review a line of argument that is so basic to the Western philosophical tradition that it has come to color much of what is considered common sense.

If you filter out the irony that runs through Plato's texts and select only those doctrines that have become identified with Platonism, you get a picture of the cosmos and the human soul as fairly neatly divided as follows. High on the order of rank is the realm of eternal Ideas: disembodied essences that define virtues like courage and justice. The human soul gains access to these Ideas by purely intellectual means—a kind of intuition that rises above all bodily contamination.

Platonism distinguishes between an eternal realm of Being, where these pure Ideas live, and a realm of temporal Becoming, where the lower parts of the soul remain mired. The acquisitive part of the soul, that part of the soul most inclined to indulge in greed, remains limited to literal perception, desire, and temporal Becoming. A higher part of the soul abstracts from the physical perception of the realm of Becoming those ideas that enable it to ascend to a nonphysical, eternal realm of Being that is free of the ravages of physical friction and decay.

Platonist metaphysics has a moral dimension that gets picked up in Christianity. It's not just a theory of knowledge that tells us how eternal ideas are abstracted from physical particulars. And it's not just a cosmology that separates physical Becoming from some sort of ideational eternal blueprint in the sky. Platonism feeds a moralistic strain picked up and elaborated upon by St. Augustine, in which the body and its physical desires are to be despised as sinful. The path of virtue thus demands the repression of desire in the name of virtue.

Picking up this antiphysical intellectualist tradition with Descartes, we find once again a slightly different angle on the same alignment of the mental over the physical, mind over matter, Being over Becoming, and virtue over vice. It was Descartes who uttered that famous dictum, *Cogito ergo sum:* I think, therefore I am. He identified the human self with its intellect rather than its desires, thereby serving as the straight man for Barbara Kruger's mordant wit that gives us T-shirts proclaiming, "I shop, therefore I am."[2]

Shopping is no laughing matter for most Americans. While grocery shopping to replenish staples ranks just above a root canal in a survey of preferences among consumers, shopping in general, along with the associated activities of consumption, absorb approximately 17.7 percent of Americans' waking hours.[3] The time devoted to shopping is lower in other nations.[4] If Americans as the world's preeminent consumers are devoting so much time to shopping and consumption, you would think that an equal proportion of theory and scholarship would be devoted to what economists call "the demand side" of the commercial equation. But no. Both supply-side economics and academic critical theory have devoted much more effort to studying creation rather than use, the active rather than the passive, production rather than consumption. "As

Andreas Huyssen has shown, in these intellectual traditions, consumption and mass culture are, in a word, feminine,"[5] and thus not as noble or heroic an object of study as the active, creative, productive side of human endeavor.

In short, many of us are ashamed of our acquisitive side. Coming at the end of a tradition that privileges form over matter, mind over body, creation over reception, male over female, we feel just a little guilty about saying that we want to consume *more*. Set against a long tradition of denial, a defense of modern consumerism might seem radical. But a solid groundwork has already been laid. Rather than claiming that my argument is all that original, I want to credit those giants on whose shoulders I will stand.

## SAVING DESIRE FROM THE INTELLECTUALS

At least since Ludwig Feuerbach, Western philosophers have begun to appreciate the role of desire as contributing to one's sense of identity. Feuerbach's famous dictum works better in German than in English: *Der Mensch ist was er isst*—man is what he eats, or, as it has made its way onto placards in health food stores: *You are what you eat.*[6] G. W. F. Hegel elevated Feuerbach's materialism to a more nuanced interpretation of the role of desire in determining the shape of self-consciousness. He saw that the desire for mere things produces a thingish ego.[7] If desire wants only things, the subject of desire will fail to hone its capacities on the spontaneous creativity of another self-conscious subject. To take a contemporary example, the desire that restricts itself to new technologies displayed in the ad pages of *Wired* magazine will remain a nerdish desire.

Hegel saw that immature consciousness becomes mature self-consciousness only by desiring the recognition of another self-consciousness.[8] The nerd must at least enter an online chat room to approach other self-conscious subjects. Sartre carries Hegel's analysis of the maturation of self-consciousness, with its dependence on recognition, into a more explicitly sexual arena where the desire for recognition turns into the desire for another's desire.[9] Here the story of desire becomes particularly interesting because, unlike a thing that I can consume and be done with, another person's desire is not something that I can master. Indeed, the attempt to master the desire of another leads straight down a long and tortuous path that French intellectuals have been plumbing ever since the Marquis de Sade rendered Hegel's master/slave dialectic as pornographic literature. As tempting as it might be to follow the French into the labyrinth of sadomasochism, I want to slow down to note how, in looking ahead to the particularly interesting dynamics of desire for another's desire, we've already fallen into the temptation that Huyssens brought to light: the temptation to attend to the active rather than the passive, the mental rather than the material. I've already followed Hegel's preoccupation with shaping and fashioning rather than the demand-side functions of acquiring, using, and consuming. To what extent might the desire for the recognition of another be mediated by one's patterns of consumption? Not to go so far as to say, "The clothes make the man," isn't it quite obvious that we are recognized by others not only for what we do or make, but also for what we have and consume?

Almost unique among theorists in attending to this humbler side of the commercial equation, Michel de Certeau has focused attention on consumption rather than production.

> To a rationalized, expansionist and at the same time centralized, clamorous, and spectacular production corresponds *another* production, called "consumption." The latter is devious, it is dispersed, but it insinuates itself everywhere, silently and almost invisibly, because it does not manifest itself through its own products, but rather through its *ways of using* the products imposed by a dominant economic order.[10]

De Certeau focuses attention on everyday activities like cooking, taking a walk, or shopping. He is interested in the ways that consumers subvert the creative intentions of producers; how they customize and alter to their own very particular ends the products and services that capital produces: "The tactics of consumption, the ingenious ways in which the weak make use of the strong, thus lend a political dimension to everyday practices."[11]

De Certeau is not Ralph Nader, however. He is not simply an advocate on behalf of consumers, protecting them from rapacious producers who would ignore the safety of their customers in the name of higher profits. As Mark Poster points out, "De Certeau's gesture is here that of the leftist intellectual rescuing from obscurity a moment of social domination. He reinscribes this moment as one of resistance 'from the bottom up.' "[12] Some of de Certeau's examples of this resistance "from the bottom up" are nonetheless drawn from contexts tailored to capture the approval of leftist individuals. He describes the techniques of Brazilian peasants using the language and religion of their colonial masters in the songs they sing to articulate their resistance. Here we have good old heroism in the name of emancipation. More interesting for present purposes are de Certeau's discourses on walking the streets of the city or shopping.

> The weak must continually turn to their own ends forces alien to them. This is achieved in the propitious moments when they are able to combine heterogeneous elements (thus, in the supermarket, the housewife confronts heterogeneous and mobile data—what she has in the refrigerator, the tastes, appetites, and moods of her guests, the best buys and their possible combinations with what she already has on hand at home, etc.); the intellectual synthesis of these given elements takes the form, however, not of a discourse, but of the decision itself, the act and manner in which the opportunity is "seized."[13]

De Certeau has cleared the ground for a study of consumption as a legitimate arena for human creativity. In order to "get down" to the level of consumer counterculture that de Certeau has delimited, we might do best to read women's magazines like *Cosmopolitan* and *Mirabella.* Or in doing so, have we not bought in wholesale to an abject acceptance of a consumer society that would allow a few to profit from hooking the many on false needs that can be profitably satisfied rather than attending to true needs that capital and its manipulation are less able to satisfy? This, after all, is the dominant complaint against *The Hidden Persuaders,* to cite the title of Vance Packard's influential book: that the success of capitalism, and the profits of the owners, turn on advertisers' abilities to hoodwink human beings into an endless rat race to satisfy false needs.[14]

Before moving on to an appropriately qualified defense of consumerism, then, two arguments are needed: first, an attack on the distinction between true and false needs, and second, a defense of the simple wish for *more.*

## THE FALSE DISTINCTION BETWEEN TRUE
## AND FALSE NEEDS

The distinction between true and false needs is one of the weaker building blocks in the edifice that was Marxism. Marx assumed that human needs were objective data.[15] The problems with this view are threefold: first, an ahistorical, biological view of human needs is inconsistent with Marx's own historicism—his acknowledgment that each successive society is the product of a self-reflexive creation of human culture by human beings. This latter historicism is at odds with any biological essentialism that would claim to define a set of real needs by reference to some ahistorical view of human nature.

Second, even if it were possible to define a set of minimal daily requirements for the human animal, the balance of evidence shows that human happiness is less dependent on the satisfaction of a basic set of physical needs than on one's perceived position on the always sliding scale of relative rank—one's relative status—in one's society.[16] This is why it does little good to say to today's poor that they have more creature comforts that medieval kings and queens.

Third, and closely related to the first two, is the view that our own self-understandings of what we take to be needs are not the simple signaling of requirements, like the blinking of an empty gas tank light from the dashboard of a car, but are always culture-laden symbolic constructs. Marshall Sahlins puts it well: "Insofar as 'utility' is the concept of 'need' appropriate to a certain cultural order, it must include a representation, by way of concrete properties of the object, of the differential relations between persons—as contrasts of color, line, or fabric between women's clothes and men's signify the cultural valuation of the sexes. The 'system of needs' must always be relative, not accountable as such by physical necessity, hence symbolic by definition."[17] This is why American baby girls *need* pink clothes.

Of course the man who has everything does not really *need* a gold-plated, automated revolving tie rack. But just as it's difficult to say where the list of biological necessities leaves off and consumer whims begin, so it is equally difficult to say where the lower limit of luxury meets the upper limit of need. Why is it so difficult? Because "human nature" is an oxymoron. To the extent that the very idea of humanity includes freedom, creativity, and the capacity for invention, to just that extent it is impossible to say, once and for all, how much is enough. We can specify minimal daily requirements for air, food, and water for the human organism, but we cannot fix the minimal daily requirements for the human spirit, because a large part of what makes us human is our capacity to enhance nature with culture, the necessary with the contingent,[18] what we *have to do* with what we *want to do*.[19]

Given this paradoxical necessity of freedom for the human spirit, it is not possible to draw a *fixed* line between true needs and false needs. Yes, it is possible in everyday, ordinary language to distinguish between those things we *really need* and those things we would *merely like,* as when one is inclined to disagree with a child who says she *needs* a chocolate ice-cream cone. But any effort to distinguish, once and for all, essential needs from accidental desires is bound to run afoul of the historical accumulation of new needs.

For example, there was a time when you did not *need* a fax machine to run a small business; now it's a necessity. I am not using the word "necessity" in a technical way, but I am not using it loosely either. Ask any entrepreneur about the need for a fax machine. A fax machine is *now* a necessity; not the sort of necessity involved in propositions like "Squares must have four corners," but a more commonly accepted, everyday sense that distinguishes the way things *must* be as distinguished from the way they just *might* be. Compared to the *current* necessity of having a fax machine, having a CD-ROM drive or a scanner remains optional. Nonetheless, I would not claim that the need for a fax machine is a "true need," not because I don't truly need a fax—I do—but because the notion of ahistorical "true needs" is inconsistent with the historicity of the human condition.

So much for "objective data" about needs. Human needs are not ahistorically determinable once and for all. Instead, they are variable in time, relative in their value, and symbolic in their constitution. One example I like to illustrate the variability, relative value, and symbolic character of needs is the need for adornment. Anthropologists tell us that, among the most primitive tribes, the apparent luxuries of physical adornment—jewelry and face painting—demand human attention before the provision of other seeming necessities like an adequate food supply or stable shelter. Hence, *Cosmopolitan* and *Mirabella* are not just icing on the latest layer of civilization; they speak to needs and desires as basic and primitive as could be.

If this first argument succeeds in doing away with an ahistorical distinction between true and false needs, what about the second argument, a defense of the simple wish for *more?* Here I want to proceed carefully because I don't want to prove too much. I don't want an argument that is so strong that it justifies greed, but I want to defend strong desire, the kind that risks crossing over into greed. Later I'll show how and why we should keep strong desires from actually crossing over into greed.

## DEFENDING THE DESIRE FOR MORE

As unproblematic as the wish for more might seem to contemporary Americans, it was not so long ago that Puritanism, as Weber pointed out, "acted powerfully against the spontaneous enjoyment of possessions whilst also [restricting] consumption, especially of luxuries."[20] Virtues of frugality and thrift had to be unlearned before the rise of the use-it-once-and-throw-it-away consumerism of the mid-twentieth century. The literature on consumer motivation is remarkably thin when it comes to any sustained and coherent accounts of the contemporary wish for more. By all accounts the classic study in the literature, McKendrick, Brewer, and Plumb's *The Birth of Consumer Society: The Commercialization of Eighteenth-Century England,* remains egregiously lacking in any noncircular account of why an active consumer goods economy arose just when and where it did.[21] Economists stress the production side of commerce and simply assume the will to consume. They take as axiomatic Say's Law that demand will always rise to meet supply. But will a soul steeped in Platonism or Puritanism rush to the marketplace?

Platonism without irony sets the soul on an upward path that would leave behind the body and its desires. Descartes, like the literal Plato, saw the physical senses as sources of deception. The oar in water *looks* bent to the physical eye; only the educated mind *knows* that it is straight. So if you want to walk in the Platonic-Cartesian path of truth and virtue, listen to your mind, not your body.

From the prospective of our post-Freudian times, the asceticism of the Platonic–Cartesian tradition looks like massive denial. Nietzsche called the bluff in *The Birth of Tragedy*. He saw the serenity of Greek culture and Socratic philosophizing as evidence for its opposite: as the triumph of Apollonian light over a repressed but ultimately irrepressible Dionysian darkness. A similar argument can be waged against the evidence of Puritanism: rather than taking its influence as evidence for the lack of the wish for more, see the need for Puritanism as evidence for the very desires that it repressed.

Freud followed Nietzsche with an anatomy of repression. And much of twentieth-century modernism, culminating in the sixties, has been a riotous celebration of our liberation from repression, a veritable Mardi Gras of the millennium. Centuries of denial give way to a *fin de siècle* delirium in which anything goes. This way lies madness. Remove the wraps of repression and restraint entirely, and unrestrained greed is the result. But does this mean that we should revert to the old basics of repression? I think not.

What's needed, I believe, is a case for exuberance, a praise of excess, but not excess excess. Not waste. Heidegger pointed in the right direction when he focused our attention upon *Sorge*, translated by MacQuarrie as *care*, but more adequately grasped as *giving a damn*. If you don't give a damn, if you are utterly indifferent, then nothing makes a difference to you and you are lost in a slough of nihilism. Nothing matters. Why get up in the morning?

Heidegger is not alone in scorning the commonplace and urging us to extremes. Nietzsche condemned "wretched contentment," and Georges Bataille insists, "The history of life on earth is mainly the effect of a wild exuberance; the dominant event is the development of luxury."[22] These citations from Nietzsche and Bataille, it might be averred, are not so much arguments as assertions. They are simply testimonials to a romantic tradition in philosophy and literature. Fair enough. But romanticism *has occurred*. And it is upon that romantic tradition that the most sustained reflection on the rise of modern consumerism lays its foundation.

In *The Romantic Ethic and the Spirit of Modern Consumerism*, Colin Campbell argues that the longing for more that motivates the extraordinary dynamism of our consumer economy has its roots in an essentially modern self-consciousness.[23] This only very recently interiorized consciousness—after all it was only three or four centuries ago that people learned to read silently rather than always reading aloud—has finally achieved the imaginative capacity to daydream fantasies that outreach the reality of our actual lives. This mismatch between our imaginative capacities and the reality of our lives induces, according to Campbell, a *longing* (I like the German: *Sehnsucht*) that is particularly characteristic of modern European consciousness.

As difficult as the term "romanticism" may be to define in terms of specific cultural movements,[24] I think we can all recognize the difference between an apathetic indifference to life and what we might today refer to as a Nike-like vigor that says, "Do it! Go for it!" We admire those who want more out of life than what many people settle for. This longing to which Campbell refers is not the same as greed, even if it can lead to greed. This longing for something more can inspire the romance of the outlaw, the Robin Hood archetype that wants more for others as well as oneself. Those who want more out of life are likely to want more out of the products they buy. The intensity of their wants translates into an uncompromising demand for quality. But it is precisely the linkage between the intensity of the wish for more and the willingness to make mischief in order to get it that drives honorable desire, from time to time, toward dishonorable greed.

Campbell's history is entirely consistent with the general thrust of my argument: that it is the work of mind that is both to praise and to blame in the several stages of the story of need, desire, and greed and that it is mind that differentiates desire from need, with the consequent good news that symbolically mediated desires are not limited to some putative set of objective, biological true needs; second (and this is the bad news), mind, as Campbell argues, can multiply our desires in fantasy to the point that no reality will ever satisfy such longing; but third, if it was mind that got us into this mess, then mind can get us out. Mind, properly informed, can appreciate some outer limits to its longing when presented with adequate evidence about the short-term and long-term consequences of its desires.

Once you abandon indifference and accept the potential agonies of caring, of giving-a-damn, then you have stepped out onto the slippery slope of desire. You have left asceticism behind and confessed your desires. Desire has been rescued from asceticism, and rather than functioning only as thorns in our sides and sources of suffering as Buddhism would have it, our desires are serving to drive our economies and shape our identities. Supported by the successes of the marketplace, the gratification of desire is etching ever finer articulations of identity: from the undifferentiated identity of "John Doe" who represents the "mass market," down to consumer segments characterized only by demographic characteristics—male between twenty and forty—and from thence, by way of the computer-driven mining of credit card records and telemarketing, to markets-of-one: just you, with your desires, your tastes, your preferences.

To follow the fractal branching of desire from the mass market through market segments to segments of one, you have to examine desire's refinement in the experience of sophisticated consumers. Once one fully appreciates the vast breadth of choice,[25] one cannot help but assume a remarkable degree of refinement and individuation of taste among consumers. For there to be a demand commensurate with the supply, the refinement of desire must equal the variety of available desiderata, and vice versa.

Inside the individual, the fractalization of desire takes the form of variations on a theme: the play of imagination using common elements in ever novel but somehow familiar patterns. The continued satisfaction of ever more relentless desire calls for an inventiveness that carves ever-finer crevices into the rock of individual identity. Charlie is not just the man who likes to fly in seat 2A (because the further forward, the sooner served, but the bulkhead lacks foot room); further, he prefers foreign cars, wears Dockers, buys a lot of mystery novels, and often eats out at Thai restaurants. What sorts of mysteries does he buy? And which dishes of Thai cuisine? These two questions mark off entire terrains for the further fractalization of desire. Following such veins of intensity you will find fanzines to satisfy every subcategory of interest, from *The Newsletter of the Barbie and Ken Fan Club* to *Model Railroaders Monthly*.

You have to marvel at the enthusiasms of esoteric collectors. Have you ever listened to two aficionados raving about the objects of their desires? Think of the gestures of an Italian tasting a fine Marinara sauce! Hear the cries of fanatic opera lovers! These are the expressions of desire's satisfaction, but not just any desires. These are the expressions of desires refined by histories of gratification that have carved deep crevices of gratification into the ever more finely articulated identities of fanatic fans. Contemporary artist Jenny Holzer created this aphorism: "Finding extreme pleasure will make you a better person if you're careful about what thrills you." It is precisely this person-building quest for pleasure that the gratification of intense desire promotes.

The fractalization of desire can devolve into fetishism, a rigid dependence on some particular pattern of excitement, an obsessive fixation on pink panties or leather straps or who knows what sexual fetish. In order to avoid the rigid dependence that is characteristic of fetishism, what is needed is precisely the inventiveness and creativity of mind: consciousness. What distinguishes desire from both need on the one hand and greed on the other is its flexibility and inventiveness, the use of mind *in the service of desire* rather than as its inhibitor. The pattern is one of successful sublimation, successful not as denial of desire but as its enhancement; mind not as master over desire but as servant of desire; superego not battling the id over what to allow the ego, but superego in the service of the id; values not as negative naughties or scolds, but values like beauty and good taste as positive enhancers of desire's satisfaction.

To distinguish sublime desire from instinct or animal need, *consciousness* is required. You have to *know* what you want. If you don't know it, you don't want it with a truly human desire. You just hunger for it like an animal. An empty cup does not desire to be filled any more than a camera is aware of the objects it captures on film. Because a camera is not conscious, it cannot even be aware. The higher level of symbolically mediated consciousness is necessary for a lower level of receptive awareness, not the reverse. Contrary to the Freudian construction, this alignment of desire and instinct runs counter to the construal of values as *constraints* on sexual or acquisitive urges. It calls instead for mind to play the role of enhancer, reflexive awareness in order that genuinely human gratification be possible at all—open-eyed and loquacious sex, good taste, sustained appreciation.[26]

Once we acknowledge the role of consciousness in distinguishing desire from need, then a number of corollaries follow in the form of a series of good news/bad news consequences. The good news: the sublimation of animal need to conscious desire means that desire is not subject to the zero-sum conservation of mass and energy—as seemed to be implied by Freud's hard disjunction between the gratification of primitive instincts or their sublimation in the works of culture and civilization.[27] In the symbolic order you *can* get more out of less. The same bits can have multiple meanings depending on context. Double entendres, jokes, and irony can multiply meanings in an endless play of ambiguity.

The bad news: this very same slipperiness and boundless infinitude is the condition for the possibility of greed. Unlike a cup that runneth over when it is full, an appetite for the sublime is not as easy to satisfy once and for all. When have you heard enough Bach? It's not simply a matter of a leaky cup that needs refilling. Instead, it's a matter of appreciating the intrinsically different logics of the physical order and the symbolic order. While need can be satisfied, desire can no more be "filled" than ideas can be oblong. Physical metaphors are misleading in the symbolic order where consciousness is at play.

The non-zero-sum logic of (conscious) desire is responsible for perpetually moving the goalposts of consumer satisfaction—and the abiding temptation to greed. For conscious consumers, there is no such thing as final satisfaction. No fixed and absolute quantity of so-called basic necessities can "fill" the hole of conscious desire. The desire for recognition and respect will lead to comparisons: no matter how much I have, how do I stack up next to my neighbor?

Once we have left behind the minimal satisfaction of animal needs, once we have acknowledged the capacity to transcend natural essence and create a new existence, then *some* degree of luxury appears to be a human necessity (as paradoxical as that may sound). But how much luxury? How much is too much? When does *some* luxury cross over into what my business partner, Stewart Brand, has dubbed "toxic wealth"?

Does this defense of desire go too far? If we have successfully transcended desirelessness, are we therefore committed to Gordon Gekko's defense of outright greed? I think not, but distinctions are in order. I want to argue for a notion I will call *proper property:* not no property (as in the poverty of communism), not the massive concentrations of property we think of as obscene wealth, but something in between. For the privacy and propriety of property to be possible, a certain amount of possessive *Sorge,* a certain amount of passionately *giving a damn* is necessary.

## THE DESIRE FOR PROPER PROPERTY

The domain of proper property covers the bulk of a bell curve that tails off on the low side toward poverty, on the high side toward obscene wealth. In order to define the domain of proper property we need not only a "poverty line" as its low-end border, but also a "wealth line" as its high-end border. Both of these boundaries are blurry, not sharp, more like the difference between a tadpole and a frog than the difference between white and black. Further, these blurry zones are historically mobile, not fixed. But like the blurry, mobile zones between youth, middle age, and old age, that blurriness and mobility need not keep us from making meaningful distinctions.

Along with "proper property," I want to coin an ugly word to capture something more complex than the desire for more consumption; I want a word that captures the desire for more-better-faster. The best word I can come up with is "consumptivity." Despite its unwieldiness (and an unfortunate whiff of tuberculosis), this word has the advantage of announcing its close relationships—its compare and contrast symmetries and asymmetries—with both "consumption" on the one hand and "productivity" on the other.

Just as productivity is not a simple idea related to an absolute amount of product, but a relational concept with a numerator and a denominator—products per worker per unit of time—so consumptivity is not equivalent to absolute consumption, but is a ratio: consumption per consumer per unit of time. This concept of consumptivity is relevant to the defense of desire bordering on greed, because both greed and desire can be expected to raise consumptivity. And why would we want to raise consumptivity? Because our advanced economies are running into problems of overcapacity, high inventories, and insufficient market demand. Declining growth rates in the advanced economies of the OECD are beginning to raise doubts about Say's alleged law that demand will always grow to meet supply. Indeed, the case could be made that increasing productivity is no longer the principal driver of economic growth in advanced economies.

In the past, when increasing productive capacity threatened to saturate home markets, the ready answer was imperialism: sell the extra inventory to the natives in the colonies. Global competition and the end of colonialism have largely eliminated that tried and true method for finding new and unexploited markets by *extensive* territorial expansion. When national economies were open systems, increased productivity could find colonial markets. To the extent that a global economy is a closed system, each increase in productivity must be matched by a corresponding increase in consumptivity. Increasing consumptivity is the postcolonial answer to *intensively* increasing demand to match supply. Increasing consumptivity will increase demand per consumer hour.

Consider as an example to illustrate this concept of consumptivity the difference between the wino and the wine connoisseur. The former may drink more wine. But the latter will do more for the economy, will employ more vintners, wholesalers, retailers, and wine writers. The wino's absolute consumption may be higher, but the connoisseur's consumptivity is higher, both by virtue of the quality of wine consumed and the quantity of ancillary demand for those who help increase the quality.

There are at least three conditions necessary for increasing consumptivity: first, the ability to consume; second, the will to consume; and third, the knowledge of how to consume wisely.

*(1) The Ability to Consume.* There is a massive paradox plaguing contemporary economics. On the one hand, we insist that macroeconomic growth depends upon increases in productivity. On the other hand, the microeconomic theory of the firm tries to raise productivity by reducing employment, which then affects the macroeconomy by reducing the ability to consume what we have produced. If we are to avoid the problems of overcapacity and underemployment, we must increase the consumerate's *ability* to consume, their purchasing power. Supply-side economics faces the following dilemma: on the one hand, raising productivity by cutting jobs leads to the reduction of purchasing power; on the other hand, cutting taxes reduces the ability of the state to restore purchasing power by the redistribution of wealth. If we want the economy (rather than the state) to do the job of raising purchasing power, then we need to find a way of accelerating the velocity of exchange by raising consumptivity to match increases in productivity. But raising consumptivity requires not only purchasing *power*, but also the *will* to consume.

*(2) The Will to Consume.* The *will* to consume is another name for desire. There are plenty of people who simply don't want much. They are reluctant consumers. You can't get them to buy things or experiences or services. Even if they have the *ability* to consume—purchasing *power*—they remain reluctant consumers. They reduce the velocity of money and restrain the wealth-enhancing capacity of the economy. Don't tell me they help the economy by increasing savings rates and investment in productive capacity. That's just another version of putting all the weight on productivity rather than consumptivity. What good

does it do us to produce more goods if they don't get consumed? Such productivity merely builds inventory, inducing overcapacity leading to subsequent plant shutdowns, fallow fields, unemployment, and the reduction of wages and the power to consume.

(3) *Wise Consumption.* In addition to both the ability to consume and the will to consume, there is the knowledge about how to consume cleanly and wisely. We need to situate our understanding of production and consumption in the context of the transition from the industrial economy to the information economy. The classic environmentalist's protest to demands for further economic growth and consumption takes the form: what if every family in China gains the ability to buy a car? Between 1990 and 1995, carbon emissions from China and India increased by 28 percent. The earth lacks the carrying capacity to allow lesser developed countries to grow along the path laid down by consumers in currently developed economies. Such economic growth is ecologically unsustainable. This third condition, this requirement for *benign* consumptivity, helps to vindicate the second and save it from attacks against crass materialism, for this third condition is a call for the sublimation of desire from consumerist materialism to consumerist etherialism. Let us distinguish the two major components of consumer materialism: on the one hand, acquisitiveness; on the other, the desire for material possessions, things, the stuff that fills closets and garages and, eventually, solid waste dumps. To the extent that contemporary consumptivity benefits from the education and sublimation of desire, consumptivity embraces acquisitiveness for proper property, but escapes the ecological and ethical perils of rampant materialism.

Does this argument put us on a slippery slope toward greed? Yes, I think it does, but there are ways to get off the slope before it's too late. How? Until quite recently, the two main exit ramps have been either an ascetic desirelessness that climbs off before the descent begins, or attacks on the very idea of private property and its unequal distribution—in the simplest contemporary parlance, the problem of haves and have-nots.

In what follows I want to take on the charge that market mechanisms are to be faulted for creating winners and losers. Even if we grant that higher consumptivity may help to produce more refined identities, are we willing to buy that gain at the cost of embracing a social and economic system that creates losers? The classic defense of the market invokes a trickle-down effect according to which the wealth of the haves will make its way into the pockets of the have-nots by virtue of another aquatic image, the rising tide that lifts all ships. I will argue that these metaphors and images do not offer an accurate picture of the dynamics of the market *today*. However accurate or inaccurate a picture these metaphors may have provided in the past, the transition from the agricultural and industrial satisfaction of biological needs to an increasing emphasis on the gratification of particular desires in an information/ services economy allows for a quite different defense of the fundamental morality of the marketplace, one that does not defend the greed of the super rich, but only the intense desire of those aspiring to more proper property.

## THE MORALITY OF THE POSTMODERN MARKETPLACE

Isn't it perfectly obvious that radical inequality in the distribution of wealth is unjust? That some should have so much and others so little? That some should go water-skiing while, in the very same frame of real-time, and connected by telecommunications that bring the horror into the kitchen on *Good Morning America,* others are literally starving to death?

But play the tape further, as the past seventy years of history have done, and you see the sequel to the impulse to egalitarian redistribution by central planners: central planning clogs the feedback loops that free markets offer for the registration of personal desires. Blinded to the individual preferences of millions of consumers, centrally planned economies blunder ahead pumping out tens of thousands of tractors and toenail clippers when what was wanted, at that particular time and that particular province, was toaster-ovens and left-handed scissors. Take away the left-handed scissors and suddenly the justice of capitalism becomes clear: except for the very hungriest who will eat day-old pizza from a dumpster, the thing that makes advanced economies go 'round is not the gnawing hunger of need but the discerning taste of desire driving consumptivity. And if an economic system cannot register the discrete desires of millions and millions of consumers, each in his or her own unique configuration of wishes, wants, and preferences, then that economic system will fail to join consumers and producers in the happy matrimony of the marketplace.

*Individual desires* are what makes the modern information and services economy sing; but the old agricultural and industrial economies are cranked to the tune of satisfying *universal needs:* food, clothing, and shelter—or agribusiness, the fashion industry, housing, and real estate. But even here, even in these ancient industries, you can see how appeals to pure functionality—form following function in the gray cement blocks of Bauhaus architecture—clog the arteries of the economy. People don't want to live in the projects. The modernist functionalist architecture of Pruitt-Igoe proved to one and all alike, from its wretched and rebellious occupants to the shocked architects and planners, that people *need* the individual differences that place the mark of humanity on the bland uniformity of necessity. Read the graffiti on the wall, comrade: the people want recognition for their differences right down to the styles of their spray-painted initials. Biological need (and note that I am not saying *true* need) may be everywhere the same; desire differentiates. All God's chillun got minimal daily requirements; only some have a taste for anchovies. Need demands productivity and efficiency in its satisfaction; the more and faster, the better. Desire seeks distinctive quality: just this, not that.

Appreciate the picture in Technicolor: the primary colors of need can paint a crude cartoon of industrial production, boxcars filled with uniform bales, container loads of mass-manufactured same, same, same. But if you want to service individual tastes, cater to the whims of discerning human beings, satisfy the fully individuated personalities of millions of self-actualized people—then you need all million shades on the Macintosh palette to color the ever-more-precisely-defined consumer segments reaching upstream to pull at the productive sources of the economy. If you bleed those subtle hues together by pushing downstream, producer to consumer, the primary red, the same, same red, the industrial mass-produced red of universal necessities, then you obliterate the information, the discretion, the discrimination, the *differences* that are the lifeblood of an information/services economy. You destroy the information that would allow that economy to function efficiently, taking tractors to the people who want tractors, nail-clippers to the people who want nail-clippers, and left-handed scissors to those lefties. The farmers don't want left-handed scissors, and the lefties don't want tractors, and without those registrations of individual desires that market mechanisms enable, the ignorant brain of a centrally planned economy can't know where to send the tractors and where to send the scissors.

In order for the central processing unit of a controlled economy to smarten up, it needs some afferent nerves. It needs to know what the people out there on the periphery of its sensorium actually desire. But in order for it to know what the people desire, it needs the information provided by the way discerning consumers make their purchase decisions in the marketplace, not just when they're standing in long lines to take anything that's fed to them, but when they are milling through the mall, picking up this, putting down that, and allowing their individual desires to *inform* the marketplace about just which colors are wanted *this* morning in *this particular* Bennetton store.

It is just this *particularity of desire,* as distinct from the *generality of need,* that makes today's advanced economies go 'round. The generality of need was sufficient to jack up the agricultural economy to the faster pace of the industrial economy. The mechanical harvester, the steam engine, and the assembly line helped to get more calories into more bellies for less time spent in the field. But now, in order to jack the industrial economy up yet another notch, beyond a speeding freight train to the speed of light, out onto the fiber-optic filaments that feed the global brain of the new economy, you have to have information about differences. And information is defined by information theorists as a difference that makes a difference, not more of the same, same, same.[28] That's redundancy, not information.

Appreciate the picture in both color and high resolution: without the information that bit-maps the precise configurations of consumer pull, you get low resolution Fred Flintstone cartoons of primitive producer push economies. In order to get the bit-map of consumer desires, though, you've got to give those consumers the opportunity to pick up this and leave that, demo this and return that, try on this, send back that. In short, you need the discriminating *retrieval* system of a market, not an ignorant *distribution* center. You need information about the consumptivity of consumer pull, not just higher productivity in the producer push.

You see where this argument is headed: in an information/services economy where marketplace mechanisms allow the forces of production to be precisely tuned to all the fine-grained vicissitudes of consumption, the unobstructed flow of information upstream, and services and products downstream, will churn with such metabolic vigor that even the least wealthy people at the bottom of the economy will have most of their biological needs and some of their favorite desires satisfied.

This is not an argument for trickle-down economics, however. Trickle-down economics rests on a fundamental error, namely, that the wealth of the upper classes, sucked as surplus value from the labors of the lowly, can rise like lava in a volcano, benefit the lofty, and then trickle down the economic volcano's steep slope to benefit the low-landers. This image of excess wealth somehow sloshing down the slopes of the economy is wrong in several ways. First, it presumes that what is wealth for one will be wealth for another, a premise that the previous argument about the particularity of desire versus the universality of need was meant to demolish. Second, it presumes that those at the top can be so completely satisfied that they will allow their *excess* wealth to splash over the walls of their mansions, a psychological assumption that proves manifestly false as soon as you observe the very wealthy and see that enough is *never* enough and that there are certain greedy people who are *never* satisfied. Third, it presumes that, even if some of this putative universal wealth were ever to seep over the walls of (unlikely) super-rich satisfaction, there is even the ghost of a chance that this molten lava will ever make it down the slope before congealing in useless boulders of solidified greed. As we well know, there are many catch basins between the wealthy and the poor. If trickle-down economics works at all, it may drip down from the towers of Wall Street to the art markets of Soho, but rarely does so much as a dribble reach as far north as Harlem or the Bronx.

We know that trickle-down economics don't work. Trickle-down economics do not provide the rationale for the morality of the market-place. Trickle-down economics are not the direction in which my argument is moving. Quite the contrary, my argument is about *the trickling up of information about differential preferences,* not the trickling down of excess wealth (whatever that might mean).

My argument rests on the proposition that, in advanced economies more than ever, the marketplace does a better job of satisfying peoples' wants and needs than any central planner. The marketplace *is good* to the extent that it *delivers the goods* to the right places at the right times. Central planning is bad to the extent that it fails to deliver the right goods to the right places at the right times. Lacking adequate information about different patterns of preference, centrally planned economies are literally ignorant. They fail to deliver the goods because they ignore the information about individual desires that is contained in purchasing patterns. They cannot *deliver* because they don't allow consumers to *retrieve* according to their own desires.

The marketplace is democratic where central planning is authoritarian. To the extent that marketplace mechanisms enhance the trickle-up of information about consumer preferences, marketplace mechanisms mimic democratic elections. The market tells the productive system what it should be producing and delivering. The market differs from democracy in that it does not guarantee everyone the same number of votes. The question is whether the market requires that there be some with no votes at all. I think not. I do not accept the old nostrum that "the poor will always be with us." I do accept that in a world of differentiated desires, differences among the less wealthy and the more wealthy will always be with us. What remains is to show how the benign effects of the increased consumptivity of the more wealthy can be prevented from tipping over into the ills of rampant greed and obscene wealth. Recalling once again that we're not looking for a fixed line but a fuzzy and mobile zone, it's time to look for the marks that would distinguish between the intense desires of those seeking more proper property from the greed of those indulging in obscene wealth.

## THE WARNING SIGNS OF GREED

Where the trickle-down argument would defend the greed of the very wealthy, the argument from the trickle up of information needs only the increasing consumptivity of those with proper property. We want to support progressive differentiation of identities, but to do so without indulging in degrees of economic inequality that are simply unjust.

Defining the obscene wealth zone—the upper rather than the lower limit of proper property—depends in part on how many people remain in the poverty zone. Surely it is unjust and inequitable to push up the obscene wealth zone when too many remain in poverty. We can allow relative degrees of more or less proper property and still reject extreme inequality on pragmatic grounds. Extreme inequality *doesn't work*—not for the very poor, obviously; but neither for those with proper property, nor, surprisingly but importantly, for the very rich. Economic analysis is now yielding evidence that extreme inequality retards economic growth overall. This is not an abstract argument about the wages of greed on the souls of the greedy, but an empirical, fact-based argument about the dynamics of extreme inequality. In one study of income differentials between rich suburbs and poor inner cities, researchers discovered that for each increase of $1,000 in the differential between mean annual incomes, those in the suburbs would eventually sacrifice $690 in income.[29] Another study based on comparisons of data from countries with a high gini coefficient (a technical measure of economic inequality) and countries with a lower (but not too low) gini coefficient shows that, over time, the latter perform better than the former.[30]

As evolutionary biologist Colinvaux argues in *Why Big Fierce Animals Are Rare,* if a species overharvests its environment, eventually it must suffer. This is why systems theorist and biologist Gregory Bateson argued that the minimal unit of long-term survival is never the single phenotype, not even a single species, but always species plus environment. Greed is so short-sighted. It doesn't work over the long term in nature. Allowing one crop to crowd out all others leads to monocultures that are far more fragile than climax ecologies that support many species.

Differentiated desires and differentials in the ability to consume can support a climax economy that serves most of its members very well. Higher consumptivity will not necessarily reduce the ratios of inequality to zero. But by accelerating the trickle up of information about differential preferences, higher consumptivity can shift the entire proper property curve toward greater wealth for all, thereby increasing the absolute amount of property, and therefore the satisfaction of biological needs of even the poorest under the property curve. Do we even want to reduce inequality to zero? I think that the fate of "the classless society" suggests not. But we can reduce the amount of gross inequality that characterizes countries like Brazil, Mexico, and, increasingly, the United States.

In addition to keeping a sharp eye on the gini coefficient of an economy so that we avoid both extremes (of low indexes like Cuba, Albania, and Sweden, as well as the high indexes of societies like Brazil and Mexico), we should also keep an eye out for the psychological signs of complete indifference to the suffering of others. One thing we can categorically condemn about greed is the way it hurts other people. And this is not just incidental. Desire wants something. Greed not only wants something; it wants what others have of that thing. It wants it back if they have it already. It wants all of what's available, independent of others' need for at least a little of it. So greed isn't just supercharged desire. Greed wants what others want and have or need to have.

Greed's ungoverned tendency to excess is what leads St. Thomas Aquinas to give avarice first rank among the seven deadly as "the root of all sins."[31] It is the sheer excessiveness of greed, its lack of a self-regulating governor, that makes it so dangerous. And yet it is the invigorating, differentiating potential of desire, and the symbolic ambiguity at the fuzzy boundary between desire and greed, that must keep us from altogether expunging greed's lookalikes from our emotional and motivational vocabulary.

## NOTES

1. See Ivan Illich, *Energy and Equity* (New York: Harper & Row, 1974); and his *Tools for Conviviality* (New York: Harper & Row, 1973).

2. See Kate Linker, *Love For Sale: The Words and Pictures of Barbara Kruger* (New York: Henry N. Abrams, 1990).

3. Cf. John P. Robinson, "As we like it," *American Demographics,* February 1993, which reports on the 1985 University of Maryland's American Use of Time Study.

4. Cf. Alexander Szalai, ed., *The Use of Time: The Use of Time in Urban and Suburban Populations in Twelve Countries* (The Hague: Mouton, 1972).

5. Mark Poster, "Michel de Certeau and the History of Consumerism," in *Cultural History + Postmodernity: Disciplinary Readings and Challenges* (New York: Columbia University Press, 1997), 122.

6. Cf. Karl Barth, "Introductory Essay," in Ludwig Feuerbach, *The Essence of Christianity,* trans. George Eliot. (New York: Harper, 1957), xiv.

7. Cf. Alexandre Kojève, *Introduction to the Reading of Hegel,* trans. James H. Nichols Jr. (New York: Basic Books, 1969), 4: "The positive content of the I, constituted by negation, is a function of the positive content of the negated non-I. If, then, the Desire is directed toward a 'natural' non-I, the I, too, will be 'natural.' The I created by the active satisfaction of such a Desire will have the same nature as the things toward which that Desire is directed: it will be a 'thingish' I, a merely living I, an animal I."

8. G. W. F. Hegel, *The Phenomenology of Mind,* trans. J. B. Baillie. (New York: Macmillan, 1949), 229: "Self-consciousness exists in itself and for itself, in

that, and by the fact that it exists for another self-consciousness; that is to say, it is only by being acknowledged or 'recognized.' "

9. Cf. Jean-Paul Sartre, *Being and Nothingness,* Part Three, Chapter Three: Concrete Relations with Others, trans. Hazel E. Barnes (New York: Philosophica Library, 1956). See also James Ogilvy, "Mastery and Sexuality: Hegel's Dialectic in Sartre and Post-Freudian Psychology," *Human Studies 3* (1980): 201–19.

10. Michel de Certeau, *The Practice of Everyday Life,* trans. Steven Rendall (Berkeley: University of California Press, 1984), xii ff.

11. Idem, xvii.

12. Poster, op cit., 121 ff.

13. De Certeau, op. cit., xix.

14. Packard's famous book is of course only one of many that have made the case that the modern consumer is the victim of overpowering manipulation by the media. Other influential works include Herbert Marcuse, *One Dimensional Man* (Boston: Beacon Press, 1964); Stuart Ewen, *Captains of Consciousness* (New York: McGraw-Hill, 1976); and author, *All Consuming Images* (New York: Basic Books, 1988).

15. Cf. Marx's *Economic and Philosophic Manuscripts of 1844,* and *Socialism, Utopian and Scientific,* together with sources cited in Marshall Sahlins, *Culture and Practical Reason* (Chicago: University of Chicago Press, 1976).

16. See not only Charles Murray's take on class-consciousness from a conservative point of view, in *Losing Ground* (New York: Basic Books, 1984), but also Tibor Scitovsky, *The Joyless Economy* (New York: Oxford University Press, 1976). See also William Leiss, *The Limits to Satisfaction: On Needs and Commodities* (London: Marion Boyars, 1978).

17. Op. cit.

18. For the most forceful arguments against the usefulness of the concept of human nature and for the ineradicable contingency at the (non-essential) heart of the human condition, see the writings of Richard Rorty, especially *Contingency, Irony and Solidarity* (Cambridge: Cambridge University Press, 1989).

19. See Brian Eno, *A YEAR with swollen appendices* (London: Faber and Faber, 1996), where he defines culture as "everything we don't have to do" (317).

20. Max Weber, *The Protestant Ethic and the Spirit of Capitalism,* trans. Talcott Parsons (London: Unwin University Books, 1930), 171–72.

21. Neil McKendrick, John Brewer, and J. H. Plumb, *The Birth of Consumer Society: The Commercialization of Eighteenth-Century England* (London: Europa Publications, 1982). See Poster, op. cit., 126–33, and Colin Cambell, *The Romantic Ethic and the Spirit of Modern Consumerism* (Oxford: Blackwell, 1987), 19–24, for detailed criticisms of McKendrick et al.

22. Georges Bataille, *The Accursed Share,* vol. I, trans. Robert Hurley (New York: Zone Books, 1988), 33.

23. Campbell, op. cit.

24. This difficulty is in part the result of the fact that the term "romanticism" has been applied to movements in painting and music as well as to literature, leading A. O. Lovejoy (in "On the Discrimination of Romanticisms," *PMLA* 39 [June 1924], 229–53) to refer to "romanticisms."

25. For example, among brands of mustard. I have it on good report that Yeltsin's epiphany, his tearful realization of what sixty years of communism had cost the Russian people, came while he was standing in front of a rack of shelves containing twenty-seven brands of mustard.

26. For a discussion of sublimation showing the contribution of semiotics to the enhancement rather than the displacement of libido, see James Ogilvy, *Living Without A Goal* (New York: Doubleday, 1995). For a very thoughtful treatment of sublimation that gets down into the details of a critique of Freud and the Freudian tradition, see Joel Whitebook, *Perversion and Utopia: A Study in Psychoanalysis and Critical Theory* (Cambridge: MIT Press, 1995), esp. chapter 5.

27. Cf. Freud's *Civilization and its Discontents,* trans. Strachey (New York: Norton, 1961).

28. For good discussions of this formulation of the informational theoretical definition of information, see Gregory Bateson, *Steps to an Ecology of Mind* (New York: Ballantine Books, 1972) and *Mind and Nature* (New York: Dutton, 1979).

29. "Hank V. Savitch, an urban policy professor at the University of Louisville, has even quantified how much the well-off lose. Suburbanites forgo $690 in annual income for every $1,000 gap between their earnings and the city's, he and three colleagues found in a study of income growth between 1979 and 1987 in 59 metropolitan areas." Cover story, "Inequality," *Business Week,* August 15, 1994. See also David Rusk, *Cities Without Suburbs* (Baltimore: Johns Hopkins University Press, 1993).

30. See Nancy Birdsall, David Ross, and Richard Sabot, "Inequality and Growth Reconsidered," for presentation at St. Antony's College, Oxford, February 1994; reported in "Economics of Equality: A New View," *New York Times,* January 8, 1994, B1, 26.

31. See *Summa Theologica,* Question LXXXIV.

# 5

## ANGER: THE DIARY

### Elizabeth V. Spelman

**January 1.** It looks as if Sloth and I are the only ones who survived last night's festivities. Greed and Lust passed out shortly after midnight. Envy began to get a little green in the gills and left just about the time Gluttony waddled in, but Pride immediately swept Big G. off in a taxi before he made a fool of himself once again with those pointless resolutions. Sloth never got around to going home—what else is new?—and I am starting the New Year as I always do, trying to figure out who deserves my wrath and who doesn't.

**February 7.** I'm beginning to feel quite envious of Laughter, especially when she's dressed to the nines to go out with Ridicule. Some of the Humanbeings seem to think that she does a better job than I do of toppling the high and mighty. Maybe they've forgotten that I'm the one who is responsible for bringing attention to injustice and other harms. Just where, I might ask, would the world be today if people laughed at things rather than got angry at them? If they just laugh, can they really think anything is wrong? And if they really don't think anything is wrong, will they try to change anything? Didn't they ever hear from Aristotle—now *there's* a Humbee who really understood me—that anyone who doesn't get angry at the right person at the right time for the right reason is a fool? Haven't they ever heard why he thought anger is an important part of friendship? Think about it: central to being angry is the belief that some kind of injustice or other serious harm is being done. So why wouldn't you be angry when harm is done to a friend

117

unless somehow you didn't care about what was happening to her? Don't leave home without me!

But, as I said, many Humbees seem to think that laughter may be a better handmaiden than I in pulling the rug out from under the puffed-up powerful. Ok, ok, the argument here is not unpersuasive. After all, like I said, to get angry at someone is implicitly to accuse him of having done something wrong (this is why getting angry at someone for something like spilling salt on the table seems unreasonable, whereas getting angry at someone for rape does not). And in one of those paradoxes that tickle so many Humbees, accusing someone of wrongdoing acknowledges or creates a sense of his importance as an effective agent, so you elevate him in the very process of trying to bring him down to size. Someone must have pretty much power to be able to do something significant enough to be thought of as "wrong" and to provoke anger to boot.

Laughter doesn't have such problems, certainly at least not when she and Ridicule are on one of their rampages. Take for instance the rapist. While I, Anger, expose him for all he's worth as an evil-doer, little Miss L. throws light on him as a sicky with a dicky, a creepy cretin whose only weapon in life is his silly member ("You call that a *what?*"). I make you see him as harmful; she makes you see him as laughable. I perhaps inadvertently accentuate his power, while she makes him wilt. Anger arms the angry person; Laughter disarms her object. Or dismembers. Ha ha.

**February 10.** I'm not so sure my envy of Laughter isn't a bit misplaced (though maybe after all these centuries of people living in fear of me I've become a glutton for self-doubt). Just the other day I was reading about a kind of Humbee called a "humorist" (no such thing as "iratists," of course—another thing that twists my wires about those dopey Humbees). Apparently Art Buchwald has allowed as how anger underlies much of his humor—and check out Molly Ivins and Barbara Ehrenreich if you have any doubts about how important anger is to their brand of humorous commentary. Ahem. But we all know that before which Pride goeth (have you ever looked at his knees?), so I better examine this a little.

Why would Laughter need Anger, and yet disguise the need? Here's why, giggle-face: Laughter needs me to pick out the appropriate objects of her attack. She likes going after injustice; but she has to be careful not to miss her mark. In that rape example I didn't suggest that Laughter made us think rape was silly; it was the rapist, not the rape, that we were supposed to laugh at. My job as Anger is to locate the injustice or wrongdoing; Laughter just handles the wrongdoer differently than I do. Humbees who praise Laughter for her ability to unplug the powerful aren't necessarily endorsing the idea that we should make anybody and everybody the object of ridicule. Ivins, Ehrenreich, or Buchwald wouldn't get very far, would they (at least not with the same batch of Humbees), if they wrote funny columns about homelessness or impoverished people, as opposed, say, to lampooning the smug consumers of beach towels from Bloomie's with "Les Misérables" spread across them in bold letters.

So Laughter needs me, counts on me to keep her attacks from being simply wanton cruelty. But why does she have to keep me in the closet? I'm so glad you asked. No doubt it has something to do with what the fact of being angry tells us about the angry person. As we know from that viciously clever put-down, "You're so cute when you're angry," to be angry is to take yourself seriously—seriously enough, anyway, to trust and perhaps express your own strong sense that something really crummy is going on. Telling someone they are so cute when they are angry is a way of trying to erase or cancel their assumption that they have the right or the ability to pass the kind of judgment on a person or on a state of affairs that being angry assumes. Laughter wants to keep me hidden because she doesn't want to come across as the heavy. Why? Perhaps—here's another nice little paradox for those chuckle-head Humbees—because the less she appears to take herself seriously, the more serious her attack will be. At her most effective, Laughter kind of scoots out of sight. It is as if the quality of being laughable is in the person laughed at, and the person laughing simply registers the facts that are there for all to see. Anger has the reputation—undeserved, if I may sniff so—for making her own presence too well known in the process of bringing attention to the unjust person or state of affairs. This may have the effect of making it look as if what the angry person attributes to the object of her anger is simply something of her own making, and not something that inheres in the object that anger notes and responds to.

In fact such a picture is suggested by a couple of familiar facts about the way we often talk about anger. Did you ever notice that at least in English there is no word that stands to "anger" as "laughable" does to "laughter"? ("Irascible," of course, won't do. "Infuriating" might do the trick if it weren't so damn hyperpolysyllabic.) We've got "you make me so angry," but that illustrates the point: it is difficult to express anger at someone without it seeming to be more about me than about him. Even though we also have "you make me laugh," this usually succeeds in suggesting that it is something in you that produces laughter in me—the plain fact of your being laughable. Notice, too, how easy it is for people who are angry to be described as, or charged with, being bitter. Indeed a tried and true way of diverting attention away from the object of anger (an attention already attenuated in ways I've just been talking about) is to quietly redescribe the person as bitter. Bitterness seems more clearly simply an interior state of the person, and a festering self-induced state at that, rather than anything like the robust response to external events that Aristotle thought of as characteristic of anger. A few years ago a Humbee of my acquaintance made clear her anger at her employer for his unfair treatment of her. Several days later a fellow worker came up and said he'd heard how "bitter" she was about how she had been dealt with. She noticed how neatly the reference to her response as "bitterness" rather than anger depoliticized the situation she was in by removing the implicit reference to a plausible reason for her feeling.

You know what that sneak Laughter is hoping I'll say now, don't you? That she is more objective than I am. That when one responds in helpless explosive laughter to a person or situation, it's not because one is irrational or blinded by passion but on the contrary is responding directly to what is there for all to see or notice. Your saying "I can't help but laugh" suggests not that there is anything amiss about you but simply that there is something out there that can't help but produce this effect in you. On the other hand the not uncommon idea that people are "blinded" by their anger implies that an angry response is an obstacle to seeing clearly, not an automatic effect of doing so, as in laughter.

I only say all this by way of trying to explain why Laughter wants to keep at bay recognition of my role in her stiletto attacks. After all, think what it would do to her claim to objectivity were my job as her head hunter and my alleged lack of objectivity kept clearly in view! Maybe this is why George Bernard Shaw counseled that "If you tell people the truth, make them laugh or they'll kill you."[1] Maybe Humbees don't go much for clear and impassioned revelations of injustice—they might have to do something about it! Maybe they find it easier to think of the world as filled with silly people rather than nasty ones. Or maybe they just think the best way to get at nasty people is treat them as if they were silly.

Time to give it a rest already. Good night, Dear D.

**March 3.** I've made myself some nice bones to gnaw on while trying to figure out my relationship with Laughter. One I can't put down is the "You're so cute when you're angry" routine. It makes me angry just to hear myself so badly misused! Plus of course the taunt all too often works just the way it is supposed to: it makes its object even more angry, now at the unjust belittlement of not being taken seriously. But I would just like to point out for the record that probably the person who says such a thing is himself angry or anyway indignant at the nerve of the other person to get angry. He may be trying to laugh at her, may even be laughing at her, but he also can't help but reveal that he finds her anger threatening. Otherwise why would he be trying to defuse it? So while on the one hand the usefulness of the taunt reminds us of why some Humbees think laughter or ridicule or mockery may succeed in popping hot human air balloons where anger might not, it also reminds us that behind such attempts at laughter lies something not at all light-hearted. It might be anger, or fear, or fear of anger. Oh damn, now I've got to think about my connection to Fear. But maybe Sloth will stop by as promised and save me. Oops, there she is now, late as usual. Mosey on in, sweetheart. The kettle is on.

**March 5.** Whew! I thought she'd never leave. I do like being around her, though; it makes me feel less riled up. In such a mood I can consider at my ease and without Consternation just what it is about me that makes so many Humbees fear me or anyway not want to be around me. What is it? I brush, I floss, I remove unsightly hair; for Chrissake I even have a couple perfumes named after me—Serious Anger, for the men, and Hysteria, for the gals—but still they treat me like Halitosis City. Of course I do know deep down what the issue is, and they do too. It really is no secret, like I said earlier, that I work for justice; ok I Lust for justice. Humbees hate being the object of anger because they know it means somebody is accusing them of doing wrong or doing dirty. (Sometimes of course they like being the object of anger for exactly the same reason.) That's why there are all those ruses I was describing earlier, all those sleights of hand to make it look as if anger is all about the person feeling angry and not about the object of her anger. If we really thought someone's anger held no implications about the object of her anger, we wouldn't be so worried about being the object. We could just say to ourselves, "Betty is angry today," in the same way we say, "Betty has a headache today." True, we might still fear that Betty would lash out at us because of her anger, just as we might because of her headache, but we could be confident that no accusations were directed our way by virtue of the state Betty is in. When Frank tells Betty how cute she is when she is angry at him, we know he's trying to change the subject, trying to shift the burden—as if all that's wrong here is Betty's insides, not Frank's deeds.

I don't mean by all this that I'm always right on target. People can get angry at the wrong person, or for the wrong reason, or out of proportion to the harm, which is why Aristotle thought it so important to get anger "right," and so easy to get it wrong, to miss the mark. But it is uncomfortable when people get angry at us even when they aren't entitled to—perhaps because we feel guilty about something we have done that they could get angry about! But go talk to Guilt about that stuff if you're interested.

**March 24.** You know, D., it isn't simply that Humbees often fear me that bothers me so much. They also tend to refer to me in disgusting or distasteful ways. Exhibit A: "I'm really pissed." In fact they seem to confuse me with various stages of watery things. Exhibit B: "Yikes is the boss ever steamed today." "Look out, Charlie's boiling." "She's been simmering over this for weeks." That's when they're not treating me like one of the other well-known elements—as in Exhibit C: "That really burns me up!" "Wow is Irma ever hot under the collar!" And oh how I wish that all those Humbees talking about "getting in touch with their anger" would find something else to do with their clammy little hands. Plus the things they say or do to one another and then use me as an excuse! You know what I mean: "I'm really sorry I called you a bitch and punched you in the face, but I was so angry I couldn't control myself." I seem to be at the top of every known list of the Basic Feud

Groups. Don't like what you've done? Just call on good old Anger to bail you out. What are they going to do if one day I blow *my* fuse?

**April 3.** And don't get me started about the "Angry White Male." Some Humbees must have paid that hussy Hypocrisy a tidy sum of money for this one. First of all, haven't most of them been saying for years, for eons, that angry people are in the throes of irrationality? (No matter that a little dose of Aristotle, a carefully drawn tincture, might have made them think twice about that.) All these centuries they've been insinuating that irrational people need to be calmed down, sedated, maybe institutionalized, listened to not to find out about the state of the world but simply to find out about the wires loose in their heads. But then along comes the angry white male and suddenly it's "Listen Up, Folks! If he's angry there must be something important going down. Let's look! What does his anger tell us about life in the United States in the 1990s?" Now mind you I don't object to taking people's anger seriously. Talk to my friends, who accuse me of droning on endlessly about how anger is no more necessarily irrational than fear is: some anger, like some fear, is irrational, but some isn't, and I've got no less than Mr. Aristotle to back me up. But I do object to the double standard that is at work when some people's anger is offered as evidence of troubled hormones, while the anger of others is read as evidence of serious grievance. But I know that strumpet Hypocrisy—I saw her slinking through town at dusk just the other evening—and how she seduces Humbees into such devilish double talk.

And this double-standard stuff is going on at an even deeper level. Do you know the enormous difficulty Black women in the United States have had convincing courts that there are some forms of discrimination experienced specifically by Black women? The courts have for the most part been unwilling to acknowledge the specificity of such discrimination. Look, they in effect tell Black women, there are other women on the job—it is irrelevant that they are white—so you hardly have a case of sex discrimination; and there are other Blacks in your workplace—it is irrelevant that they are male—so there are no grounds for a charge of race discrimination. As one judge put it, recognizing a form of discrimination specific to Black women would open up a veritable Pandora's box (where has the Cliché Patrol been on this one?), and the indefinitely large number of permutations and commutations of cases based on people's multiple identities would keep the court dockets filled till the end of time. (Interesting, isn't it, that as early as 1790 those assiduous census takers in the US of A wanted to know whether residents were "free white male," "free white female," or "slave.")

Thus it is just about impossible for Black women to bring discrimination suits before courts of law, because they must show that they are discriminated against either because they are women or because they are Black, but not because they are Black women.[2] Meanwhile, that *other* intersectional group, Angry White Men, don't even need courts to recognize and understand their plight: somehow lots of Humbees can't get their heads around the idea of Black women being discriminated against as Black women, but they seem to understand perfectly well what it is for white men to feel aggrieved as white men. Note that the angry white man is not just a man, race unspecified, or even a white man, emotional state unspecified. He's the angry white man, in whose name not too long ago both Democrats and Republicans were bemoaning how skewed so much of public policy has become. And so while focusing on the specific condition of Black women in the United States, perhaps especially poor Black women in the United States, is taken to be proof positive of one's having caved in to treacly, fuzzy-headed PC thinking (except when accusing that particular group of being welfare queens), focusing on white men, more particularly angry white men, is taken to be a sure sign of having one's finger on the serious political pulse of the nation. No matter that we were supposed to be worried about the Pandora's box of complex identities; no matter that last time we checked, anger was associated with irrationalty. Angry white men are serious business, bub.

Oops, the fax machine has started to purr. Forgive my fickleness, dear D. Catch you later.

**April 5.** Sorry for that interruption, but for once it was worthwhile: Gluttony let me know he was going to be sashaying through town and was eager to take me out to dinner. (He spends a lot of time with Greed and as a result is used to picking up the tab. I wasn't about to protest.) We went over to that nice spot on Alighieri Boulevard. I ordered my old stand-by, Penne Peccata, and the more adventurous G. tried what turned out to be a delicately seasoned breast of Penance Under Glass. We split a bottle of the '72 Pinot Purgatorio, which was out of this world.

**April 7.** So, dear D., my point was not that I mind people thinking of anger as something to be taken seriously. *Au contraire,* as my cousin Colère used to say. But as I said I don't like it when Hypocrisy offers my services to those who use the fact of being angry to write off some people as nutcakes and at the same time to bring attention to other people as seriously aggrieved. True, amongst the flurry of newspaper and magazine articles about the Angry White Male in recent years, there are some complaints that referring to these white men as angry is a pejorative way to describe them—implying that anyone with a really serious grievance shouldn't be described as angry. But in the main, recognition of their anger has been a way of taking them seriously, and the only debate is over how seriously. Notice that these guys aren't referred to as "bitter," or "petulant," or "whiny," or "whimpering," nor, for God's sake, as "irrational,"[3] let alone "hysterical" or suffering from a hormonal imbalance. And nobody seems to have talked about how cute they are when they're angry—although after Oklahoma City you can see why. But what about Laughter and her gang? Where have they been? Perhaps scared off by a scold writing for the *Wall Street Journal,* and I quote: "If the [Oklahoma City] bombing does, in fact, represent the ultimate expression of angry white male frustrations, those on the political left will respond by merely mocking those frustrations. That is precisely the wrong reaction."[4] Gee, just when we had finally learned that it is only feminists who don't have a sense of humor, just when the *Wall Street Journal* and other organs of political righteousness had convinced us that only the hyper PC among us worry about hurt feelings. Please, when it comes to Angry White Males, no laughter! This is *serious.*

Now don't misunderstand me. I don't doubt that Humbees have a lot to learn from studying the phenomenon of white male anger—including what they might gain from reflecting on the denial that the men in question really are angry. Their being angry is simply a "myth," one columnist insisted.[5] How do we know that? Well, white males who voted on election day 1994 were asked by various pollsters if they were angry, and anywhere from 70 to 80 percent of white males said they weren't. Geez, when did Humbees ever come to think that the best way to tell whether someone was angry was to ask them? Most of the time, though, the fact of their anger wasn't questioned. But there was much rummaging around to find out just what they were angry about, or whom they were angry at, and the thought seemed to be that finding that out would be instructive for the American public. The general consensus seemed to be that they were angry about losing jobs, or not getting them to begin with, and about what they saw as unfair policies that put them in such a precarious position; they were angry at governing bodies that developed and enforced such policies and the non-white non-male people who presumably got the jobs that surely belonged to them. Well I just think it would be very interesting to think about what they didn't get angry about, who they didn't get angry at. We didn't hear much about their getting angry at CEOs who may make up to 200 percent more than they do, nor about having been brought up in a society that taught them that being white and male was ipso facto such a guarantee of blessedness that they needn't think about the unmentionable meaning of class in US history. Maybe they *should* be angry. Maybe they just should think a little more about for what and at whom.

**May 7.** I should stop playing those trivia games with my nephew Ira. Yesterday he caught me completely off guard when he asked which group sang "You Can't Always Get What You Want." I could have sworn it was the Grateful Deadlies, but he said wrong wrong wrong and relieved my wallet of a five-dollar bill. However the whole affair did make me start thinking about whether I *do* get what I want, which in turn made me wonder if I even know what I want. My shrivener—that's "shrink" for you pagan infidels snooping around in my diary—asks me at least every other week "What does Anger *really* want?" (I wonder, just by the bye, whether Lust and Envy are ever asked the same question.) I sometimes think he's accusing me of being promiscuous—as if he couldn't possibly understand why someone whose calling in life is to bring attention to injury and injustice wouldn't be found longing to be in the arms of Apology one day, Punishment another, and Revenge on a third. What I "really want," my sweet confessor, depends on my sense of the nature of the damage done and what it would take to repair it. If occasionally I appear to want to exact more from the wrongdoer than appropriate to the harm, well sorry sorry sorry, I guess I'm more human than I thought. Bug off.

**May 11.** Get a load of this, Dear D.! You remember that Greed didn't accompany Gluttony when he popped into town several weeks ago? Well guess where the old Grabmeister was. At one of those Virtue Conventions—you know, a gathering for Humbees all hepped up about other Humbees' nasty ways. Our very own Greed, it turns out, is nobody's fool. He knows there is BIG money in the Virtue business and has wormed his way into becoming a close confidant and consultant for a prominent Virtue Maven—someone who used to be what the Humbees call a "professional philosopher" but for many years has been refining his talents as professional scold while occupying high if nonelective political office, and now has published himself into existence as the Czar of Virtue. Greed has enough discretion and loyalty to refer to his new pal only as "Big Boy," and enough of a sense of irony to enjoy the spectacle of B. B.'s making money hand over fist by extolling the virtues. (Oops, those Virtue folks don't like the word "fist"—it makes them think you are talking either about revolution or kinky sex. Which reminds me that I want to continue that conversation with Lust about whether there is no one with a more prurient imagination than the person who rails against prurience.)

**June 2.** If Greed can make a few bucks in the back rooms of Virtue Conventions, maybe I could too. Pride of course has always been welcome there, knowing as well as he does the utter shamelessness of Humbees who like to parade their virtues around. I've been thinking about hawking my wares there—selling some of those pretty little baskets I've been making over the past few years. I figure that if Humbees really think of me and the other members of the Gang of Seven as deadly rather than merely cardinal sins, then maybe I should try selling one of those Handbaskets in which people go to Hell. Actually I'm beginning to like it—A Streetcar Named Desire, A Handbasket Named Anger . . . not bad, huh?

**June 13.** Now Dear D., please pardon me for returning to a certain pet peeve of mine, brought on by all those recent thoughts about Hell, Relation of Deadly Sins To (see also Purgatory), and Hell, Going in a Handbasket To. Lots of Humbees seem to find it hilarious to be told ad nauseam something to the effect that Hell Hath No Fury Like a Woman Scorned, or is it Spurned, or maybe Burned. Whatever. I'm not about to give away any secrets about Hell, but I notice a very slick piece of sidestepping going on: any dolt who reads the police blotter can tell that Earth Hath No Fury Like a Man Left. I daren't pick up something like the *Boston Globe* (we're not talking tabloids) over a meal any more, for fear of tossing up my tofu over the most recent story about some guy whose girlfriend or wife decided she wanted out of the relationship: if he can't have her, well, nobody can, and he'll make sure of it by eliminating her, and then if possible for good measure he'll include any children or grandparents in the vicinity. Then maybe to show how sincere he is, he does himself in too. Ok, I know this is not a laughing matter. I'm just wondering about all the clever devices Humbees have developed for ignoring life-threatening forms of anger that seem the inevitable accompaniment to the idea that you can own other people or their bodies or their affections. And instead of blaming just me, they might think about the part Pride, Greed, and Envy's first cousin Jealousy play in all this (don't believe all that stuff about such violence being a matter of Lust).

**June 19.** Unfortunately for my reputation all those clichés about Hell Hath No Fury Like dot dot dot seem to make Humbees question my pedigree: is she really from the House of Justice, as she likes to pretend? or does she just not understand the difference between justice and vengeance? aren't she and Outrage from the same litter?

Well, I must say I'm rather flattered (yes, Pride has had his way with me, too) that Humbees seem to have been trying to get their little cheeseheads around this one for ages. Long before Aristotle tried to set them straight, tried to get them to see the difference between appropriate anger, on the one hand, and its deficiency or excess, on the other, there was Aeschylus's account of the Furies in the *Eumenides*. It's not a bad portrait. Some people have wondered why there are three of me—just like they wonder why there are seven of us Deadlies—and while I am not about to reveal state secrets, I must say I can't deny reports that the three Furies (Tisiphone, Megaera, and Alecto—apparently the first incorporated law firm) morphed out of Father Heaven's genitals after one of his sons, Cronus, sliced off them there private parts and tossed them into the deep blue sea (I am not making this up).

This purported genealogy of the three Furies may simply be the figment of Lorena Bobbitt's ancestors' imagination, but that is not really my point. Aeschylus's picture of the Furies provides a very helpful account of my complicated but crucial connection to justice. As I seem to remind you several times a year, Dear D., I like to think of myself as lusting after justice—*but*, as you also would be the first to remind me, sometimes I get a little sloppy, a little too hot-headed, and confuse my real goal with sweet swift revenge. Well early in the *Eumenides* the Furies are hot on the trail of Orestes, who has murdered his mother, Clytaemnestra, in retaliation for her having murdered his father/her husband Agamemnon and then having set up housekeeping with another gent. Clytaemnestra thought Agamemnon had a thing or two coming his way for having sacrificed their daughter, Iphigenia, and then having returned victorious from war ready to install another woman, Cassandra, in the house he shared with Clytaemnestra. You get the picture. The Furies appear to be hell-bent on getting Orestes to pay back in agony the agony he has wrought. "We track them down" is their motto—along with "We brook no trial." (In the movie version I saw, the Furies were played by Bette Davis, Joan Crawford, and Margaret Thatcher). There ends up being a trial, however, with Athena presiding, and while technically the Furies lose their case—as any dodo knows, it's worse for a wife to murder her murderous philandering husband than for a son to murder his murderous philandering mother—Athena sweet-talks them into hanging around as a force for good rather than continuing in their destructive ways.

With the Furies Aeschylus suggests that real justice emerges when powerful sources of revenge are acknowledged and can come to be persuaded that there is a calmer, still passionate but more appropriate role for them to play in responding to generations of terror and bloodletting. So, although at the beginning of the action it seems as if justice and vengeance are two quite opposite and mutually repellent forces, by the end we learn that they need each other—kinda like justice without vengeance is empty, vengeance without justice is blind.

The argument needs some fine tuning (hey it's a play not a philosophical treatise), but as I said I think as Humbee accounts of Anger go this one does a good job of capturing my intriguingly complicated nature. The *Eumenides* provides a rich dramatic analog to Aristotle's somewhat later, drier profile of my personality: Anger properly understood is certainly not a force of pure rationality, but neither does she have only irrationality coursing through her veins. Anger is a living, breathing example of the forces of irrationality at work in company with reason. Reason without passion is empty, passion without reason is blind.

As Aristotle said, and I like to repeat perhaps rather too often, anybody who doesn't get angry at the right thing for the right reason at the right time is a fool, isn't properly disturbed by what is going on. In portraying the Furies as in need of some maturing, as coming to be transformed not by being bludgeoned into submission but by listening to and being persuaded by calmer heads, the *Eumenides* prefigures Aristotle's explicit teachings about how people have to learn to be angry in the right way (though Aristotle seemed to think that only non-slave men could do it). It's hard. No one is born knowing how to do it, and it is far from an exact science. But there are plenty of wrongs in the world, and Anger is a crucial companion for those who want to make sure they are righted. You may find me a little humorless (*vide* my eternal competition with Laughter), but trust me, compared to the Furies in their unregenerate stage, I'm a barrel of fun.

**November 29.** Just back from our family reunion, which we decided to have this year on Thanksgiving Day. Probably a mistake, since most everybody seems a little long in the face. Envy hasn't been able to get rid of that problem with bad breath. Lust is balding at an astonishing rate. Gluttony has had to have another round of periodontal work. Sloth is getting bunions. Greed is being audited by the IRS. Pride's face-lift didn't set in the way he hoped. Me, I can't complain: since my rehabilitation, business has been booming, and my relationship with Mirth is going quite nicely. If I'm not careful I'll have to cancel that long-term contract with Piss & Vinegar. Toodle Doo.

## NOTES

1. Quoted in Claudia Roth Pierpont, "The Strong Woman. What was Mae West really fighting for?" *The New Yorker,* November 11, 1996, 106.
2. See especially Judy Scales-Trent, "Black Women and the Constitution: Finding Our Place, Asserting Our Rights," *Harvard Civil Rights-Civil Liberties Law Review* 24 (1989); and Kimberlé Williams Crenshaw, "Demarginalizing the Intersection of Race and Sex: A Black Feminist Critique of Antidiscrimination Doctrine, Feminist Theory and Antiracist Politics," *University of Chicago Legal Forum* 139 (1989).
3. However, the implication that *Black* men who are angry might well be irrational is very apparent in pointed references to "intelligent black male anger." See Letters, *Newsweek* (International Edition), October 21, 1996, 12.

4. Gerald F. Seid, "Making Sense of Angry Males and Extremism," *Wall Street Journal,* April 26, 1995, A16.

5. Charles Krauthammer, "Myth of the Angry White Male," *Washington Post,* May 26, 1995, A27.

# 6

# LUST

## William H. Gass

My desires were never allowed to reach the lust level. That doesn't mean I don't know what lust is, for lust is an essential ingredient in life. Like most of the vices, lust is fundamental and necessary. Deep down it is a virtue, whereas the virtues themselves are surrounded by vices as boxers are by their sycophantic sponging entourages. This is why people with lots of "faults" are often loved, and why saints are despised while they live, frequently tortured to death, and admired only after they have expired.

Just as there are the greater and the lesser Antilles, so there are greater and lesser virtues. Neatness is one of the latter, and a handy example. The neat person believes that there is a place for everything and that everything should be in its place. The neat person is an enemy of history, erasing evidence of every party, pretending nothing happened—especially lust. Few things are sexier or more inviting than a rumpled bed. Neat people are fascists of the mop and bucket, the tight sheet, the silver chest. They never use the good dishes. They like the way it was yesterday. The order that neat people prefer is not creative; it is stifling. We need neat people, but only a few at a time. To pick up in parks.

Truthful people are a big pain. That is their aim in life: to be a big pain. Because we naturally love lies. Lies are more fun, far pleasanter to hear for the most part, and certainly more effective. In fact, they are called for. Parents pretend they want to know whether Gertie is screwing in the parlor and if Peter is smoking pot in the barn. And if the kids tell them the truth, they will be ragged and snagged and grounded unmercifully. So the kids learn. Lying promotes freedom. Lying guards privacy. Lying saves lives and wins elections. Of course, we need to be truthful, but only on occasion.

I am talking, of course, about the little lies of daily life, not the big lies of priests and politicians, those who want to fix things and those who want things fixed. Lutherans, for instance, don't like lust. Catholics and Calvinists are both against lust. Mormons allow us several wives but it's not on account of lust. Baptists are not on lust's side. If you measure a man by the quality of his enemies, Mr. Lust does well.

The trouble with temperate people is that they are rarely temperate. All the temperance societies I know promote abstinence. "Nothing too much yet everything a little bit" is not their motto. No. Nothing is the operative word. Masturbation in moderation is not their motto. A truly temperate person doesn't play golf every day. A truly temperate person doesn't run more than a block a week. Temperate persons eat sensibly, which means they never diet. But professionally temperate people only worry about sex and alcohol, drugs and atheism. Professionally temperate people are cranks. Atheism they ought to like. Atheists admire the word "nothing." But they probably don't admire lust much. Not a single favorable vote from the Methodists. Pietists—nix.

Piety is a nasty little virtue. Reverence for Pa the father, Ra the god, and hurrah the flag. Piety is respect for power and privilege, ancestors and their dead-and-gone deities. There is nothing in the world worth worship.

Adultery, on the other hand, cannot be too frequently practiced. If adultery were understood to be a virtue, and committed whenever opportunity offered, then we'd soon be unsure whose kid was whose, the hierarchical character of families would be disrupted, and the succession of paternal property would not succeed. Lust would be at last separated from the coarse and common activity of begetting. Going to bed with one person for the rest of your life? You've got to be kidding. Kidding . . . yes, kidding is the problem.

So what about lust? Let's compare it with gluttony. That will get us off to a good start. Satisfied lust isn't fattening. Satisfied lust may mean two people are happy. "It's the restiest thing thar are," Granddad used to say. It improves the skin, all that blood rising to the top like cream. It detenses the limbs so that all one's aches feel far away and in the past. Common courtship costs. You take one another to dinner, gluttonize, pay up, the heart burns. But lust is easily relieved without any outlay. You can easily eat too much, grow round as the earth, break wind, ache, but there is no penalty for coming twice. Sexual satisfaction raises self-esteem, produces a healthy languor, and leads to a happy life.

Lust is, of course, the sexual impulse dialed up. So that one is alert and on the search, one feels encouragingly alive, paying attention to one's friends and companions because they may relieve the itch. Which is after all better than no attention at all. There are always those undiscovered chests, those untouched tummies, the straits of paradise.

Why would one want to put a stop to it?

There are practical reasons: babies, diseases, babies. But these problems can be readily solved. There are other things at stake: patrimony, power, possession, pride. Anyway, it isn't lust that is really being proscribed. The aim of lust's enemies is to deny lust its satisfactions. Lust is thereby exacerbated, strengthened, multiplied.

Let's go back to the beginning.

God walks in the Garden to enjoy the cool of the evening. God makes clothes for Eve and Adam. God savors Noah's sacrifice. The smoke of a good goat. He has to descend from Heaven to check out the Tower of Babel which is rising toward Him and would reach Him if He'd just wait. He is his own investigative team looking into the alleged criminality of Sodom; however—hey, what's going on?—He has permitted the Snake to Inhabit Paradise. Moreover, He misrepresents the consequences to Adam and Eve of eating the fruit of the tree of knowledge. He is jealous that Adam and Eve will become gods like himself. I think He envies their nubility. After all, Isn't He the Ancient of Days?

God has one law, never mind how many the lawyers manage: obedience to the commands of God. That's why the laws must be accounted equal. For the same reason that Zeus cuts the round people in half, according to Aristophanes in Plato's *Symposium;* and God scatters the language of Babylon hither and yon, destroying their unity along with their tower; God also punishes Adam and Eve for not doing what they were told. Hubris is at the root of it. Man may have been made in God's image, but he is only a faint and distorted reflection. He dare not presume to rival his father and get to know what's going on.

What sort of knowledge of good, and what sort of knowledge of evil, results from eating the forbidden fruit? Is it knowledge by acquaintance, so that suddenly Adam and Eve lust after one another and go to it in the bushes? Is it knowledge by description—equivalent to reading a self-help book on how things are done? Is the knowledge basically, as some think, of practical matters: the way God's creation works, and how Adam and Eve can now command its laws; or is it more narrowly the inexperience of innocence destroyed by disobedience and disobedience followed by shame, work, and death? The Garden was The Good Life. It sheltered the bliss of ignorance. Adam and Eve didn't know that either, although their subsequent exile—their sojourn in an evil world—is a condition whose character they now know well.

It was the juice. They bit into the fruit, and, as Rainer Maria Rilke wrote, life and death entered their mouths. They tasted culmination. They ate what surrounds seeds. The fruit hid inside its succulent skin—an apple, a pear, or a peach. They awoke within these sensations. Lust sang inside them like a bird. And they saw they were naked.

The serpent, or jinn of the tree, never struck me as more than an ordinary con artist. The Devil dwells in this story's interpreters. Their motives, one and all, were malignant. It is they—the St. Pauls of this world—who give lust a bad name. Sexual feelings and their consequence recapitulate the fall and pass sin on, as miasmas were passed, from generation to generation. The act of making more men and women makes the men and women made genetically wicked. This doctrine creates a world of customers needing to be saved. Lust is thus the core feeling that inhabits all wrongdoing because sex is its symbol.

Women are secondary creatures. Women are weak. Men who obey their wives are in deep trouble. Women must endure the pains of labor as a punishment for the sexual pleasure they probably never received. Adam and Eve were perfect because they were begot by God and thought, therefore, they might be gods, whereas their descendants have . . . [insert an exception for Mary] . . . mothers.

Over time, people were encouraged to forget that disobedience was the original sin (Satan's *non servlam*) and to believe that sex was the evil agent. Adam and Eve were as little children romping around the plastic kiddie pool until some mom or pop began to make them put bras and panties on. And the apple got blamed. Not the pear. Not the peach. Not

the grape. But there were those—there always are—who argued that
the tree was a vine, and that the serpent offered Adam a glass of wine.
Well, it was the juice.

There is no need to dignify this malicious little tale with any further
interpretation. It simply became a useful moment for those seeking
power to reinforce their views. Encased in a sacred text, guarded by a
pampered priesthood [insert an exception for saints], its allegorized message became central to Christendom's traduction of our sexual lives.
Lust, which ought to be the feeling of life itself; erection and reception,
which ought to be creative signs in whose physical exemplification pure
delight is taken; the closeness passion insists on, whose loving intimacy
of touch ought to yield the reassurance of one's acceptance; the ecstasy
of release and its resulting relaxation which should yield a sense of security and peace and serene renewal: all these gifts of nature to us were—
not only by organized religions, but through cultural policies both social
and political, and by the pandering of profiteers and traders—made to
blush, to seem evil, low and nasty, at worst like our fecal necessities—
though obeyed, never displayed, praised, discussed.

"In their zeal," Rilke writes of believers in "The Young Work-
man's Letter," "they do not hesitate to make this life, which should be
an object of desire and trust for us, bad and worthless—and so they hand
over the earth more and more to those who are ready to gain at least
temporary and quickly won profit from it, vain and suspect as it is, and
no good for anything better." (The C. Craig Houston translation.)

Not only do these liars promise to rescue our souls from the ground
where our bodies rot, they tell us our human nature and all the signs of
life in our species have put us there, into the dirt we deserve. So if we
give up life here, we may later have it given back to us up there. How
stupid we must be to believe in that promise; to accept the honors af-
forded chastity, for instance, that prolonged and perverse denial of our
present existence; to reject this world for a nonexistent other.

Of course when lust must go about in black clothes and seek other
outlets for its energies, in power and privilege mostly, or ally itself with
pain and pursue its infliction, or substitute shopping or golf for its goals,
growing moist only at the mention of money, getting hard at the prospect of rape or war, then lust will be called "lust" and be regarded with
loathing and fear, and lust will be said to be selfish and interested in its

own satisfactions, and sexual organs will be places where favors are sold and money is made, not where joy is experienced; then lust will have to seek permission for its satisfaction by obtaining a license to drive from the State, permission to mate from the Church, and approval from Family, Friends, and Credit Card Companies, but only to make babies and go into long-term debt.

Lust seeks another; lust is inherently social. Frustrated, arousals unanswered, the masturbator is sad and alone. Your own hand is not a fun date.

The lustful gaze—that great look on life that says, "I want it, it will please me, I shall please it in return, we shall merge more usefully than vehicles on the highway, we shall experience the interiors of one another, we shall burn like painless fires"—is thus not meant for men or women alone, and not perversely for vacuum cleaners or sheep, but for the sensuous appearance and shape of things, for the taste of fruit, the feel of silk and leather, for songs in another's throat, for a horse in stride, and strong rich lines of verse.

Lust is present in any desire that has a strong sensuous component, because lust rises from form and color, and moves closer for odors to count, and then for taste and touch to fulfill it, for it's not orgasm lust lusts for, but the juice of the orange squelching between the teeth, the touch of an inner thigh that transforms the palm, the smell of stew in a winter pot, snowflakes melting on glowing cheeks, wine rinsed meditatively in the mouth, the sound of an ah! after a long in-drawn breath.

To realize one is naked, rather than just one of the other girls and boys in the plastic pool, is what kind of knowledge? Is it knowledge of good and evil, or is it awareness of opinions fabricated by a society that has its reasons for lying and pretending and faking it. Adam and Eve saw they were naked; they saw they were naked because they saw, at the same time, that nakedness was wrong; they saw it was wrong because the tree of knowledge was put up by a Santa Claus working for the Salvation Army.

Certain of our needs have a small range of satisfactory solutions: for thirst, water is the first and last solution; everything else we might drink—pop, juice, Scotch, soup—will be useful only because of the water it contains. For thirst, water is reality. Hunger, on the other hand, can be satisfied in a thousand ways, most of them by food growing in a distant country however, by mythological beasts, by paying a high price. Even so, there is always a significant number of choices.

So those who dominate the value choices in our societies, whether they represent Business, State, or Church, always try to regulate diet, clothing, off-duty activity, and sex. Eat veg, wear black, pray while standing on your back, don't have fun: don't dance, don't hum, don't fuck from the rear, don't suck anything, don't handle yourself or anyone else, don't enjoy, don't smear fluids, don't shout or move a lot.

Hide her behind veils, voluminous folds, body paint, high walls, patriarchal laws, cut her clit, or her hair, slit her nose, trade for cows—these are sins—not a nipple reaching its full height in another mouth. Not babytime down south. Burn her alive along with the furniture. Bury her in your tomb, you stiff. Slice her heart out with a sliver of stone. These are sins. Sliding out and in is just plain nice when it's done because it's just plain nice. Hey, at my wedding car, don't throw the rice.

> You think it horrible that lust and rage
> Should dance attendance upon my old age;
> They were not such a plague when I was young;
> What else have I to spur me into song?

("The Spur," from *New Poems* 1938)

Old man Yeats knew what was true. If you have no anger at this world, anger at its willful stupidities, its grim indifference, its real sins: its many murdering hordes, its smug myths, exploitative habits, its catastrophic wastes, the smile on its hyena's face, its jackal tastes; then you belong to it, and are one of its apes—though animals should not be so disgraced as to be put in any simile with Man.

Old age ought to know. Death will soon enough come to its rescue. Till the knowing ends, all that was wasted and wronged in youth—through ignorance, haste, competition, bad belief—all that was bored by middle age into one long snooze has borne its juiceless fruit and is now known for what it is: nothing has been righted here. Yet if desire can be kept from contamination, if it can be aimed, as one's fingertip, at the root's place, if it is not harnessed to the horses of dismal domination, but is allowed to be itself and realize life; then the flutter of an eyelash on a cheek will assume its proper importance; Wall Street may crash and the gods of money be smelted back into the sordid earths they came from; yet unfazed, our heads will rest at least on one another, a fall sun will shine on the sheets, your nipple shall enter my ear like a bee seeking in a bloom a place to sleep; life shall run through us both renewed; we shall feel longing, lust for one another; we shall share rage for the world.

# 7

# ENVY: POISONING THE BANQUET THEY CANNOT TASTE

## *Don Herzog*

I nsidious gnawing envy, the vampire vice: it creeps up unawares, surprises us, grabs us and sucks up our cheerful energy, our very willingness to get out of bed and perform the day's allotted chores. Envy has been nominated—Lord knows it isn't alone, but the case is perfectly plausible—as not just the worst vice, but the most insistent, along perhaps with lust, relentlessly preying on our consciousness, preoccupying us during the day, making us toss and turn when we seek sweet repose, even torturing us in our dreams. Worse, it looks more or less coextensive with social life itself: or at least there are plausible, even powerful, reasons to suspect it's inevitable. There are others out there, after all, and their presence forces one to raise unseemly questions. How good are you, anyway? Or, to acknowledge the hallowed case facing generations of tortured adolescent males confronted with the most menacing site in high school, the dread locker room: How big is yours? How big is his? Why does she seem so charming in groups while you mumble and fumble and humiliate yourself? He got promoted!—how could he? that undeserving worm, he just sucked up to the boss, never had a good idea in his life, while you sit in your dusty cubicle unappreciated, unrecognized, unaffirmed. Such questions, however embarrassing to pose, seem thrust upon us by the task of working up any account of who we are, where we stand. For how else could we figure that out but by comparing ourselves to others? To be a self, to have an identity, is already to have a story about where you stand in all kinds of pecking orders.

Worse, these unseemly questions might have unseemly answers. Maybe yours isn't very big, is embarrassingly tiny in fact. Maybe she is genuinely charming and you are an oaf, a boor, a philistine, whose nominal friends barely suffer your presence. Maybe you are rotting neglected in your cubicle in accordance with the transparent dictates of ruthlessly impersonal meritocracy. And now you've got to live with it. So the very process of working up an account of yourself, of becoming a self in the first place, has left you damaged goods, nursing a wounded self, maybe nursing some grudges, too. How could it not? Did you expect to find yourself at the top of every hierarchy, well endowed physically, a master of the social graces, professionally accomplished, with a poignant touch on the violin to boot? No, not even in your most audaciously arrogant moments.

But surely not everyone is envious. Shamelessly lapsing into autobiography, I offer not just a ritual protestation of innocence, but a wholly sincere and heartfelt confession: I myself am not at all envious. I find it easy to rejoice in the accomplishments of friends, to admire my superiors, to ponder others' valuable accomplishments without feeling diminished. Now, does this mean I'm suitably secure, that I enjoy the goods of self-respect and self-esteem? That instead of moving against others, seeing them as hostile rivals, I generously move toward them, seeing them as incipient friends?[1] Or does it mean I'm actually oblivious, to their accomplishments or my own emotions, that I'm kidding myself? Or that I'm insufferably arrogant?

My own predilections aside, and more seriously: The problem of ever-beckoning envy is exacerbated by so-called positional goods, goods like honor whose possession consists in one's having more than others. Here your gain has to be my loss. But arguments for the inevitability of envy don't require positional goods. Consider Jesus's parable.[2] Early one morning, workers agree to a day's labor in the vineyard for a penny. All day long, the owner hires additional workers, promising that "whatsoever is right I will give you." At day's end, to the consternation of those who've worked the whole day, everyone earns one penny, even the workers showing up at the eleventh hour. So they grumble: "These last have wrought *but* one hour, and thou hast made them equal unto us, which have borne the burden and heat of the day." Leave aside Jesus's moral—"the last shall be first, and the first last"—and the trouble it's caused over the centuries for its mystified and appalled audiences. The employer appeals to the norms of contract: they agreed to work for a penny and that's what they're getting, so what's their complaint? They think he's unfair, of course, but they may also envy those who had the good fortune to show up late. (Or, thinking about the parable's implications: what is the lifelong Christian, devout from his childhood to the bitter end, supposed to think about the miscreant wretch who devotes himself to wine, women, and song, and converts on his death-bed? and the extra joy the angels greet him with? Just that it would be imprudent, given the contingencies of timing surrounding death, to take a chance on having time left to convert?)

Back to the vineyard. We needn't assume any positionality—there is no evidence, say, that the vineyard's owner has a fixed amount of money to offer as wages and is committed to distributing all of it—but it's perfectly natural for those who showed up in the morning to be grumbling. A deal that would have left the workers hired early in the morning perfectly happy is spoiled by the greater good fortune of others: marvel at the psychological alchemy that takes one's happiness, adds another's happiness, and combines them into misery. The envious have a knack for creating misery ex nihilo, for making themselves and others worse off than they need to be. In a shrewd French medieval romance, St. Martin happens upon a covetous man and an envious man. Being a saint, he instantly detects their vices. Not the most benevolent saint in the annals of Christianity, he makes a canny offer: whichever one asks for something shall receive it; the other shall receive twice as much. The covetous man hangs back, thinking to cash in more splendidly. Yet the envious man pauses—he "dared not to ask according to his desire, for reason that he feared to die of grief and malice that his comrade's portion should be larger than his"—until, threatened with a whipping by the covetous man, he lights upon a satisfactory solution. He asks St. Martin to remove one of his eyes—"very careful was the saint to observe his covenant"—so the covetous man is left blind.[3] We are to presume that the envious man would rather have two eyes, but he can't stand the thought of the covetous man having more goodies than he does. But would the envious man prefer that they'd never stumbled across cursed St. Martin? Do the pleasures of not having to envy the covetous man, of pushing him down, even of exulting in his tragedy, more than com-pensate him for the loss of his eye? And is the moral of the story that envy and covetousness are both vices? or rather that saints are not one might imagine or even hope?

Anyway, the very fact of social life, the inevitable comparisons one draws—or has drawn for one, by cheerfully malicious onlookers, their tongues dripping acid or their pens stabbing malice—doom one to envy. And envy dooms one to misery. But are these causal connections necessary?

Envy has a history. Not just the objects of envy, though they register the remarkable inversions and confusions of Western cultural change. Today it's mildly embarrassing, if not worse, to inherit the Rockefeller fortune, to know that birth alone entitles you to such magnificent wealth. People might envy you the brute fact of the wealth, but *you* are more enviable if you are the original Rockefeller, if you earned it yourself: leave aside hesitations we might have about just how the old man clawed his way to such a fortune. In the *ancien régime*, though, the *nouveaux riches* are incurably vulgar, and the most enviable fortune is the one stemming back centuries. Recall Pooh-Bah: "I am, in point of fact, a particularly haughty and exclusive person, of pre-Adamite ancestral descent. You will understand this when I tell you that I can trace my ancestry back to a protoplasmal primordial atomic globule."[4] But also the scope of envy—the referent of the concept—has a history. I want to suggest—and even offer some impressionistic evidence for the claim—that over the centuries envy has been pared away, leaving a pointedly unpleasant core.

From the first, the Western literary tradition testifies to the sickening paralysis of envy. The envious consume their own vitals. Ovid has the goddess shut away in a gloomy cave, munching on poison. When Minerva visits her—this is Addison's translation, eloquent in its way if a bit mannered for us—she staggers forward:

> Soon as she saw the goddess gay and bright,
> She fetch'd a groan at such a chearful sight.
> Livid and meagre were her looks, her eye
> In foul distorted glances turn'd awry;
> A hoard of gall her inward parts possess'd,
> And spread a greenness o'er her canker'd breast;
> Her teeth were brown with rust, and from her tongue,

In dangling drops, the stringy poison hung.
She never smiles but when the wretched weep,
Nor lulls her malice with a moment's sleep,
Restless in spite: while watchful to destroy,
She pines and sickens at another's joy;
Foe to her self, distressing and distrest,
She bears her own tormentor in her breast.[5]

So too *Piers Plowman* personifies Envy as pale, sickly—"in the palsy he semed"—his wan cheeks making him look like a leek left out too long in the sun. Repentance urges that sorrow will win him salvation, a bit of piety earning this bitterly dry response:

"I am evere sory," quod [Envye], "I am but selde oother,
And that maketh me thus megre, for I ne may venge."[6]

That is: he always regrets his own envy, which leaves him so skinny, is so enervating, that it prevents him from taking revenge on those whose good fortune so tortures him. "Envy is . . . its own Punishment; a Punishment so great, that when a man becomes extremely Envious, it even pines him away, it wastes his flesh, consumes his bones, eats his very heart," agrees a seventeenth-century preacher.[7]

Envy might not scale such anorexic heights. It might even come with pleasures attached: think of scratching an itch, picking at a scab, thrusting your tongue into a cavity, leaning hard on an arthritic joint. You can get warm and cozy with your envy, nurture it anxiously over the years, cuddle up with it for bitter consolation, just as you can with your neurosis. But these are dubious pleasures. So now we have this cheery line of thought: social life consigns us to interpersonal comparisons, which consign us in turn to feeling crummy about ourselves, which in turn is paralyzing. Maybe we should enlist this as indirect support for Nietzsche's equally cheery maxim, "action requires the veils of illusion."[8] Only those with robust self-esteem can act, but only those deluding themselves could enjoy such self-esteem. The envious can console themselves with the thought that they at least see the world clearly—and as Nietzsche notes, such knowledge breeds nausea. So is such clear-sightedness enviable? or is it a curse?

Yet does social life really doom us to anything so sickening? You look around and find yourself wanting. Need you waste away? I suppose not. There are in fact a cluster of possible responses, only some of them, to our way of thinking, envious. Instructively, though, some of them historically have been taken as part of envy. So consider:

## EMULATION

Your lack is energizing: you get off the couch and start working at realizing the good you envy in another. This is emulation, and described this way we're inclined to approve of it. So Thomas Elyot in 1541 has the emperor Alexander, oozing unctuous virtue, repel the suggestion that an illustrious family lineage (or "auncient nobilitie") is required for one properly to serve the state as a distinguished office-holder. Alexander wants someone, illustrious or not, "in whome sinceritie and temperaunce be joyned with wysedome." "If he be but late come to worshyppe," that is only recently distinguished, "his aduancement shall ingender in noble men an honest enuy, eyther to excede hym in vertue, or at the leste to be iudged equall unto hym."[9] The crucial adjective *honest* is there to save this sort of envy from being relegated to the ash heaps of repulsive vice. Maybe that makes us doubt its credentials as envy, but maybe instead it should make us ponder the sordid motivations driving some of our best efforts. It's one thing to realize that someone else's accomplishments are inspiring, to rededicate ourselves to the pursuit of excellence. It's another to take their accomplishments as an affront and pursue excellence as a kind of revenge: "I'll show you," we mutter darkly, "you're not so hot, I could do that myself." Alas, it's easier to draw the distinction between these two sorts of emulation on paper than it is in the world. They often run together: take the case of keeping up with the Joneses. ("The Joneses got a new car today," trilled the Temptations in the '60s; "here's what you should say: 'Hurray for the Joneses!' But instead you worry, till your hair turns gray. . . .")

So we have norms to guard emulation, to try to fence constructive admiration off from unhealthy revenge (not to mention self-deprecating sycophantic imitation). Imagine a skater—call her Tonya Harding—who wants to be the best skater in the world and wants further to be publicly recognized as the best skater. Say she wants to win an international competition—call it the Olympics. She practices, hard. And she surveys the competitors. How does she react on discovering another skater—call her Nancy Kerrigan—who not only seems to boast the antiseptic good looks of a refined mannikin, looks adored by skating judges, but who seems like a damned good skater in her own right, maybe a better one? Harding isn't permitted to realize her ambition by, say, hiring someone to crack Kerrigan's kneecaps. She can practice, practice, practice; she can try as hard as she can; and then, when she loses, we demand that she grin cheerfully before the TV camera, with all its cruel publicity, and acknowledge Kerrigan's excellence. We even demand that Kerrigan be demure, that she generously applaud her competitors' ability. The poise we impose on her is so demanding that we wouldn't let her whimper if someone were to assault her kneecaps.

Contrast the overgrown babies of the *Iliad*. Famously wronged by Agamemnon's seizing a sexually desirable woman for his own prize, Achilles does what any spoiled brat would do: he goes and pouts—actually, he sobs—and refuses to play any more. We're sometimes told that Achilles never exacts revenge, that this is a sign of his noble detachment from the pettier side of heroism. But in fact there's a nice quiet moment of revenge in the athletic competitions the Greeks stage to show off their prowess after defeating the Trojans. These heroic athletes have no poise, no dignified restraint, whatever: they exuberantly scramble to claim their prizes and vaunt in them, just like poorly socialized children who triumphantly rip off the gift wrap at their birthday parties without even glancing at the cards. A newly wise Achilles, inspired by the realization that death strikes everyone alike to think that there's something deeply phony about honor and glory, still knows how to tweak the local understandings of competition and excellence. So when Agamemnon rises to demonstrate his prowess in archery, Achilles instantly calls off the competition and awards Agamemnon the prize: everyone already knows how good you are, he tells a stunned Agamemnon.[10] This isn't an especially vivid form of honor. It deprives Agamemnon of an opportunity to do a glorious deed, to strut his stuff, to win the envy of the other Greeks. And that envy is a coveted prize, maybe *the* coveted prize, of honor.

## SCHADENFREUDE AND SPITE

Hobbes has already pared off emulation from envy. "*Emulation,*" he holds, "is grief arising from seeing oneself exceeded or excelled by his concurrent, together with hope to equal or exceed him in time to come, by his own ability. But, *envy* is the same grief joined with pleasure conceived in the imagination of some ill fortune that may befall him."[11] Taking pleasure in others' failures looks on its face like the converse of envy. But one medieval source after another sweeps it in under envy's scope. Envy, we learn in "St. Edmund's Mirror," is "Ioye of oþer mens harme, and sorowe of oþer mens wele-fare." The Mirror goes on to say something less jarring to modern ears: "Envye mase men to have þe herte hevy of þat he sese oþer men mare worthi þan he in any thyng."[12] But the Mirror isn't abruptly changing the subject. The heart that's heavy seeing other men more worthy in anything is the motive for a certain kind of *Schadenfreude*. Not the snicker that greets the pompous speaker who rises to the lectern with resolute gravity, oblivious to the lobster bisque splattered across his tie: so much doesn't require any antecedent envy. But suppose you previously had noticed to your dismay that he cut a more imposing figure in public than you, that the thought rankled, and that now you rejoice in seeing the fates bring him low precisely because his humiliation makes him less of a threat to your self-esteem.

What about not just chuckling over others' downfall, but aiding and abetting it? "Cinderella" has been nominated as the quintessential fairy tale of envy, the plot allegedly driven by the stepmother and stepsisters' envy of Cinderella's native superiority.[13] I always thought the story was an attempt, like so many others, to glue together natural refinement and social hierarchy: Cinderella's exquisitely tiny foot, badge of dainty refinement, destines her for the royal family. And I always thought the stepsisters too blankly stupid and wooden to aspire to anything as intricate as envy. Surely envy's home in the fairy tale is that creepy incantation, "Mirror, mirror, on the wall, who's the fairest of them all?" Not enough for the evil queen to be singularly attractive. She has to be the single most attractive. This lofty aspiration leads her not just to solicit murder, but it makes her ugly: remember her disguise as the gnarled old woman selling apples. It's the same transformation marked by pale palsied Envy in *Piers Plowman*.

Bacon takes lashing out in spite to be partly constitutive of envy. "Deformed Persons, and Eunuches, and Old Men, and Bastards, are *Envious*: For he that cannot possibly mende his owne case, will doe what he can to impaire anothers. . . ."[14] Bishop Butler agrees: "To desire the attainment of . . . equality or superiority by the *particular means* of others, being brought down to our own level, or below it, is, I think, the distinct notion of envy."[15] So too Dr. Johnson insists that most malevolence stems not from selfishness but envy: "most of the misery which the defamation of blameless actions, or the obstruction of honest endeavours brings upon the world, is inflicted by men that propose no advantage to themselves but the satisfaction of poisoning the banquet which they cannot taste, and blasting the harvest which they have no right to reap."[16]

In a haunting bit of early Soviet fiction, one character summons up a childhood memory of a little girl. "She was the queen. She did whatever she wanted, everyone admired her, everything emanated from her, everything drew towards her. She danced, sang, jumped and thought up games better than everyone else." He had his own claims to social grandeur, as a record-holding gymnast: "I, too, had become accustomed to rapture, I, too, was spoiled by worship." Elaborate and nefarious social codes, already mastered by children anything but innocent, destined them to be partners. But she spurned him. Enraged, he lashed out: "I caught the little girl in the corridor and gave her a thrashing, tore off her ribbons, let down her locks into the wind, scratched up her charming physiognomy. I grabbed her by the back of the head and knocked her forehead against a column several times." At least in recollection, he understands full well what he was about: "At that moment I loved this girl more than life, worshipped her—and hated her with all my might."[17] That is, he was powerfully drawn to what was valuable in her but simultaneously repelled by its being hers. Not that all these traits could have been his: some were feminine, after all. (A heterosexual man might envy a woman her being found sexually attractive; but could he envy her her hourglass figure?) He thought he would degrade her status, but of course he degraded only his own. Here we are beyond anything recognizable as *Schadenfreude*—too much active malevolence for that—and into spite. But, however tempting such fantasies of spoiling the valuable other, the envious need not be spiteful, need not even gratify themselves in *Schadenfreude*.[18] They can just sit, paralyzed, and stew in their misery.

## SOUR GRAPES

Aesop's fox has an elegant solution—maybe an enviable one—to the problem of wanting something he can't have: he downgrades its value.

Aesop also imagines a caterpillar envying the colossal length of a snake. "Wishing to match length with the snake, he dropped down beside him and tried to stretch himself until he strained so hard that, before he knew it, he burst."[19] This caterpillar, convention has it, needs to recognize his own nature. But suppose the caterpillar were to deal less self-destructively with his envy by jeering at length and pretending to pride himself on his diminutive stature. Could he succeed? It depends in part on how well entrenched is the social code defining length as more valuable. Maybe he could hunt around and find some reference group willing to affirm his quirky defense of smallness. Maybe they could team up against the lofty long snakes of the world. (Some such account helps motor Nietzsche's account of the triumph of slave morality.)

We're tempted by sour grapes more than ever. A society showering us with more possibilities than we can conceivably pursue makes us free. But every time we make a choice, we renounce indefinitely many other possibilities. Or, if you like, sculpting one's life means murdering thousands of counterfactual selves one could have become but has chosen not to. What one renounces has genuine value: thus the queasy sensation of loss, of regret, and thus the baleful glowering we do at others who have blithely affirmed the very alternatives we have renounced. Now imagine that the path you've chosen has turned out badly and they are flourishing—precisely as you could have flourished. "What an idiot I am!" you exclaim, clapping your forehead in dismay. Or, with a touch of *mauvaise foi* you hope will become deeply sincere the longer you indulge in it: "What idiots they are!" Just sneer at them, the drones, stupidly taking the easy way out; better, surely, to be the noble failure you are. And what makes you think your course was any nobler than theirs? Just that you've failed in it.

If we are forever reminded that our choices are contingent, there's something mechanistically simple about the economist's thought that we could define equality as an envy-free distribution of resources. For sometimes my envy will attach to your resources just because they're yours. (And I will downgrade my own resources just because they're mine, my diseased self-esteem blessing me with a perverse Midas touch that cheapens everything I touch.) If we carved things up again so that we were indifferent between the two bundles of goods to be portioned out, I could nonetheless come more or less instantaneously to envy the bundle you get. "But you just agreed it was no better than yours!" Sure, but that was before *you* got it. "But you're not being rational!" Sez who?

## RESENTMENT

Which is worse, knowing that your rival deserves her success or knowing that she doesn't? The tradition is torn here. One ancient text, long but mistakenly placed in Aristotle's corpus, forthrightly holds that envy is for another's undeserved prosperity.[20] "Envy," declares Adam Smith every bit as forthrightly, "is that passion which views with malignant dislike the superiority of those who are really entitled to all the superiority they possess."[21] Suppose you stew over your rival's winning the promotion you so desperately sought, and suddenly you realize that she's more talented than you, more industrious, and that the boss made the right call. That's one pain, one kind of self-diminishment. And it can feed on itself: suppose you reproach yourself for feeling bad about her deserved success; now you have to come to terms with the further news that you are the sort of worm who would feel bad about something like that.

But suppose she's less talented and industrious than you and the boss, incompetent wretch, has bungled yet again. During high school and college, I worked summers in an above-ground swimming pool store. The manager, astoundingly incompetent, had literally come with the building: there he had formerly managed a toy store for the building's owner, who either chose to overlook that his manager's incompetence had driven that operation into bankruptcy or became a landlord protecting his bozo manager's job with a fiendish chuckle of revenge. It was easy enough for me to laugh at his blunders: I was just amassing a bit of cash to help my real quest, piling up cultural capital. In fact his bizarre incompetence was reassuring; it reminded me that this wasn't my real life, that I was headed elsewhere. Those actually working for him couldn't merely laugh. Here, detachment saved me from fury. Misanthropes who cultivate a general sense that the world is a feast of misrule, fools at the helm everywhere, gain a blanket salvation from such fury: just one reason that misanthropes enjoy serenity.

So is this clueless manager enviable? He is after all excellent in his way, the clown prince of ineptitude, with no rivals on the horizon.

Okay, you don't want to be clueless yourself; but do you want to be the lucky SOB who cashes in with not even inconspicuous merit of your own? We often pine for a world in which everyone gets what she deserves. In doing so, we slip into preening ourselves on all the good things rightfully headed our way. Whatever strands of self-esteem we uneasily command prevent us from noticing balefully all the good things we don't deserve, from rejoicing that theodicy remains a fantasy.

John of Salisbury glosses envy as "the moroseness that originates at sight of the prosperity of another." But not, he immediately adds, if the other is "a tyrant or wicked citizen," his prosperity undeserved.[22] (I assume this is John's inference. But what if the tyrant happens to be a virtuoso on the flute and the crowd's applause isn't caught up in fear of his political might?) Then you are not envious but resentful, not vicious but a righteous agent denouncing patent injustice: Rawls draws the same distinction.[23] Once again, the verbal distinction is sharper than the actual emotional terrain. St. Edmund's more parsimonious gloss—envy is sorrow of other men's welfare—doesn't distinguish resentment from envy for good reason. Resentment can be fueled by envy, by the wounds inflicted by the brute fact of the other's superiority, deserved or not, wounds quickly commanding the language of moral indignation and injustice, accurate or not.

Desert is too narrow a category, actually, to capture the wondrous variety of ways we can afflict ourselves in envy. Suppose your brother has a chiseled chin: he didn't work for it, say by dieting frantically and overcoming the family tendency to obesity that you, like a slug, have succumbed to. (What if he purchases his chin, literally, by paying for plastic surgery? That's shabby. But what if he wasn't wealthy and had to scrimp and save for the operation? May he now celebrate his chin? Or does that make him even shabbier? But what if we transform him from your brother into your sister: do the gender norms excuse or even justify the pursuit of good looks under the knife? What if the sister isn't in the clutches of those norms, happily, even mindlessly, identifying with them, but grimly decides it's too costly not to capitulate to the absurd beliefs of others?) He was just born lucky, inheriting the same little cluster of genes that Clint Eastwood has cashed in on. ("Hey, pal," he quips, "whatcha doin', envying me my chin? You've got three of your own!") Your brother isn't a movie star, but he too cashes in, as the good-looking usually do, in one social setting after another, effortlessly charming men and women alike—and all because of the shape of his jaw and the small amount of adipose tissue lurking around it. Surely he doesn't, strictly speaking, *deserve* his chin. Even his claim to deserving the cascade of nice things that depend on the chin is shaky at best. But you might not envy him the nice things; you might just envy him his chin. It's his and it's valuable, after all, even if he doesn't deserve it. Or envy might follow the trajectory of *eros* in Plato's *Symposium*: its object might initially be the brother or the chin or the good fortune flowing from it, but finally it might attach itself to something like disembodied value, along with a haunted sense that you yourself are shorn of such value.

Theorists of social justice often imagine, complacently, that they are also giving us the grounds of self-esteem. Quite the contrary: they are ushering in a world of untold envy. Suppose you're not making it in an unjust society. Then at least you win the booby prize: you get to be a fierce prophet of indignation, a voice of morally self-assured resentment. But suppose you're not making it in a just society. Now careers are open to talents, primary goods distributed to maximize the position of the worst-off, and so on. Now you have no one to blame for your failure but yourself, and that will fester. The same social justice is likely to turn the prosperous into arrogant twerps, sanctimoniously self-assured in the knowledge that they have fairly earned what's theirs. Better, surely, that they have some uneasy guilt and anxiety about whether they can rightfully claim their good fortune as their own. If the price of justice is priggery, is it really worth it?

Emulation, *Schadenfreude* and spite, and sour grapes, we now think, are possible responses to envy, not partly constitutive of envy itself. Resentment is another matter altogether. Again I want to suggest that we can learn something from the more expansive scope the concept once possessed. We can learn to scrutinize with a bit more jaundice our motivations in trying to excel, in chuckling at others' plights, in dismissing certain traits or activities or possessions as not worth having, even in denouncing unfairness. In the meantime, though, we've pared envy down to that sick paralyzing sense of despair, the tormenting blow to self-esteem suffered at the realization that someone else is better off.

I doubt that that core sense has shifted all that much historically. True, our ways of discussing it have changed dramatically. But—to take the quintessentially modern version—Freud's penis envy, enough to leave certain women in the pricey throes of analysis interminable,[24] looks rather like a flat translation of some Christian homilies. (But doesn't penis envy offer a distinctive theory of the genesis and object of envy? I suppose. It also invites its mischievous counters: I know two girls who have worked up a theory of vagina superiority, commiserating with their father over having to stuff his genitals into his pants or having them wobble around. A familiar psychoanalytic riff allows us to transform this intriguing theory into its humdrum opposite and thus enlist it as further support for the master's views, out of the mouths of babes: but I wonder.) So too, and more strikingly, Melanie Klein's ruminations on the infant's encounter with the good breast and the spoiled breast, deeply formative infant experiences leading individuals to trust or suspicion, happiness or sadness, calm security or raging envy, though always with the possibility of later working things through and finding reparation and wholeness.[25] If we read them as allegorical—I mean that strictly speaking, as allegorical as the quest of John Bunyan's Christian—they recapture ancient and Christian wisdom; if we don't, they inspire skepticism.

What about the pleasures of being envied? Can you buttress your self-esteem, your affable contentment in being you, by feasting on the sight of those stricken with envy at your success? Finessing the usual rivalry among fellow literary stars, Pope wrote to Addison, "I am so far from esteeming it my misfortune, that I congratulate you upon having your share in that, of which all great men and all the good men that ever lived have had their part, Envy and Calumny."[26] The syntax is complex, and not just because of the baroque cadences of Pope's vintage early eighteenth-century English. Why does Pope have to rebut the view that Addison's suffering the envy of others might count as Pope's misfortune? Wouldn't a devoted friend take that line? But the envy Addison suffers is—just tweak the word choice a bit—the envy he enjoys, or should enjoy. He is to be congratulated on it. And it is then Pope's good fortune too: he assures Addison that he takes pleasure in Addison's victory. He could, after all, be envying Addison the envy Addison is getting from others ("would that I were envied as you are!"). And which does—or should—Addison want: Pope's rejoicing or Pope's gnashing his teeth in envy? Piety demands that if he's Pope's friend, he wants Pope to rejoice.

But maybe knowing that you've earned the envy of your friends is especially delicious.

If there's room for prickliness here, it's because Pope and Addison are not just friends but also rivals for the esteem of the reading public. When we envy others their superiority, Hume reports, "'tis not the great disproportion betwixt ourself and another, which produces it; but on the contrary, our proximity. A common soldier bears no such envy to his general as to his sergeant or corporal; nor does an eminent writer meet with so great jealousy in common hackney scriblers, as in authors, that more nearly approach him."[27] Mandeville puts the point with characteristic acerbity: "If one, who is forced to walk on Foot envies a great Man for keeping a Coach and Six, it will never be with that Violence, or give him that Disturbance which it may to a Man, who keeps a Coach himself, but can only afford to drive with four Horses."[28] One might have thought that the pedestrian has more to complain about and so more grounds of envy, but his social distance dulls the passion.

Put differently, rough equality enables the possibility of envy: you don't consider envying those too far above you. (Can you envy those ostensibly beneath you? Sure: take the tortured genius who wishes now and again he was mildly dumb, the overworked senator who wonders whether his secretary's life is better than his, the second-grade teacher who would on mature reflection rather be a second-grade student. But such cases feature people questioning the conventional hierarchies. Maybe the second-grade teacher has come to see aging as decay, those bright-eyed innocent youth as the peak of creation. Regardless, surely you don't envy those too far beneath you.) It just doesn't occur to you that you could ever be in their position. Gazing back fondly, Tocqueville readily acknowledges the "inequality and wretchedness" of the glory days of feudalism. But he assures us that "the serf considered his inferiority as an effect of the immutable order of nature," so it didn't degrade his soul.[29]

Here envy lives a political life. Usually, though, the claim is not that equality creates envy, but that envy creates equality. A gargantuan and insanely repetitive conservative chorus since Tocqueville have assured us that the demand for equality, for democracy, is nothing but an expression of base envy. Leftists, the refrain goes, are tortured by the sight of superiors and wish to drag them down. And equality can be nothing but such leveling.

My favorite rendition is a 1961 short story by Kurt Vonnegut.[30] "The year was 2081, and everybody was finally equal. They weren't only equal before God and the law. They were equal every which way." The United States Handicapper General, pursuant to the 211th, 212th, and 213th amendments to the Constitution, has an ingenious battery of devices designed to prevent the superior from taking advantage of their superiority. Smart people wear "a little mental handicap radio" whose bursts of noise prevent them from thinking too well. The beautiful wear ugly masks. And so on. But even in this cowardly new world, envy hasn't quite been eradicated. Mediocre Hazel contemplates her brainy husband George's handicap radio: " 'I'd think it would be real interesting, hearing all the different sounds,' said Hazel, a little envious."

There may be people who join the left because they are envious. (I myself don't know any.) But suggesting that that is the sum and substance of the matter boggles the mind. To say the screamingly obvious, leftists are intent on raising the position of the worst-off, not dragging down the superior. No one ever said that Boston Brahmins shouldn't be allowed to attend fancy universities, for instance; people struggled instead to make higher education available to whole classes once excluded from it. To be just a bit less obvious, there are millions of conceivable—and actual—motivations for supporting equality. Take Bernard Shaw's acidulous comment: "Class hatred is not a mere matter of envy on the part of the poor and contempt and dread on the part of the rich. Both rich and poor are really hateful in themselves. For my part I hate the poor and look forward eagerly to their extermination. I pity the rich a little, but am equally bent on their extermination."[31]

The conservative idea that the demand for equality might be impeached as a cloak for envy is best taken as a reminder of how stupid political ideologies can make us. One sociologist embarked on the remarkable project of grounding all of social life—and especially the stupidities of the left—in envy.[32] More recently, right-wing journalists have attributed the increasing acrimony of the relationship between American blacks and Jews to black envy for Jewish achievements.[33] Never mind that Jews were already far better off than blacks in the '60s, when relations between the two groups were far warmer. These political theorists of envy are in the clutches of an idea powerful enough to prevent their noticing minimally obvious facts.

The closer people become, the more salient otherwise imperceptible differences become. No wonder the medieval Christian writers worried so about envy: they knew the hazards of monastic life, with those nuns and monks in their identical uniforms, equal servants of God with lots of time on their hands, crankily observing who received slightly warmer smiles, whose voice lilted a tad more musically in devotions, and on and on. The social organization of devoting oneself to serving the divine was a breeding ground for one of the deadly sins. Put differently, the quintessential home of egalitarian envy isn't the Soviet Union or Sweden's social welfare state; it's the priory.

I return to the bleakly plausible line of argument of my starting point. Envy is born with social life itself, with working up an account of who you are and how you stack up. Or the possibility of envy: for it isn't really true that envy is inevitable. How might it be avoided?

The Christian sources urge not just that we love our neighbor, but that we cultivate humility. Augustine is unflinching about what devotion to the city of God entails: love of God, up to and including contempt of self.[34] A slightly cynical reading would be that we are enjoined to drive our self-esteem so pathetically low and to focus our attention so singlemindedly on God that we're incapable of aspiring to anything as elevated as envy. A suitably humble self isn't sickened by the sight of prosperous and happy others, as remote as Tocqueville's nobles from his serfs—or horribly misguided about the true ends of human life, and so in fact despicable, objects not of envy but of pity. Or if it is sickened, it takes the further flagellation as cause for worthy spiritual discipline, the old Adam within erupting yet again.

I suppose we secular humanists are more inclined to urge the merits of a reasonable pride—don't feel so bad about yourself, we counsel the envious, you're not so bad—but that's just to parry one sin with the thrust of another. (Whatever sense we can make of the unity of virtues—not much, in my view—the unity of vices seems hopeless on its face.) Or consider Sir Philip Sidney's *Arcadia*, a best-seller in England for many decades: "Those who have true worth in themselves, can never envy it in another."[35] But how do they know they have true worth? Can any solitary individual just announce firmly that he's worthwhile regardless of what others think? No: but Sidney imagines aristocrats with a bold disregard for what most people think. (We are vanishingly close here to Socrates's characteristically charitable reflection in the *Crito* that most people act at random: so why care what they say?) They limit the reference group whose approval they depend on. But then aren't the whole gang of them invidiously proud? even haughty and contemptuous?

Or consider the possibility of renegotiating the grounds of self-esteem. Take the egalitarian standard of doing the best that you can. Sam might bowl an effortless game of 225 while Tim struggles to reach 160, but Tim needn't envy Sam's ability. In fact, if Tim has tried harder, his effort is more admirable. There are further curious wrinkles here: if we are prone to applauding effort, we might grin approvingly at Tim ourselves; but who would we really rather be? Did "We Try Harder" get people to shift their business from #1 Hertz to #2 Avis? Did it make them feel any wistful affection for Avis? or just unmitigated contempt? Why do Americans root for underdogs? Is it because the fans secretly believe that they themselves are losers in the game of life, so they thrill to the thought that their counterparts might somehow prevail?

Even if it doesn't make envy inevitable, social life remains full of pitfalls. Over the centuries, self-appointed wise men, Epicureans and their many followers, have advised us to shun the world of competitive posturing, to beware positional goods, to mind our own business, to withdraw. So Voltaire's Candide, ruefully reflecting on the travails accompanying his quest, ready to retire from the world and its commotion, fends off his tutor's mechanically repeated mantra that still this is the best of all possible worlds with a biting rejoinder: "we must cultivate our gardens."[36] The allure of beneficent nature, far from the madding crowd: here is peace, here is solace, here is joy, here is loneliness: away with envy.

But never fear! Envy awaits you even in your garden. A recent issue of a periodical aimed at flattering the not-so-elderly into feeling rather too terribly good about themselves asks—implores—the reader, "Want to Create Tomato Envy?" A full-page photo boasts a man preening on a stepladder, a woman with a knowing smirk on her face, both posed in front of a tomato that's preposterously larger than they are. "Here's the dirt," proclaims the teaser headline, "on how to grow the biggest and tastiest."[37] A snug and comfy retirement, indeed, underwritten not just by the largesse of the federal government and the indefatigable lobbying of the AARP, but also by basking in the pain of one's neighbors, knowing that they confront their own sickly garden specimens with newfound dismay. What more zesty seasoning for a tomato? or a life?

# NOTES

Thanks to Phoebe Ellsworth, Bill Miller, Martha Nussbaum, Bob Solomon, and Andy Stark for comments.

1. Here I draw on the structures in Karen Horney, *Neurosis and Human Growth: The Struggle toward Self-Realization* (New York: Norton, 1950).

2. *Matthew* 20:1–16.

3. *Aucassin & Nicolette and Other Medieval Romances and Legends*, trans. Eugene Mason (London: J. M. Dent, 1910), 129–31.

4. Gilbert and Sullivan, *The Mikado*, act 1.

5. Ovid, *Metamorphoses*, bk 2. I assume this is the ancestor of Shakespeare's "green-eyed jealousy" in *The Merchant of Venice*, act 3, sc. 2.

6. William Langland, *Piers Plowman*, 5.077–5.127.

7. Jonathan Blagrave, *The Nature and Mischief of Envy: A Sermon Preach'd before the Queen* (London, 1693), 14.

8. Friedrich Nietzsche, *The Birth of Tragedy*, sec. 7.

9. Thomas Elyot, *The Image of Governance* (London, 1541), 77 recto and verso.

10. *Iliad*, bk. 23, ll. 890–94.

11. Thomas Hobbes, *Human Nature* [1651], in *British Moralists 1650–1800*, ed. D. D. Raphael, 2 vols. (Oxford: Clarendon, 1969), 1:9. Contrast Hobbes, *Leviathan*, chap. 6.

12. "St. Edmund's Mirror," in *Religious Pieces in Prose and Verse: Edited from Robert Thornton's MS.* [*circa* 1440], ed. George G. Perry, rev. ed. (London: Kegan Paul, Trench, Trübner & Co. for the Early English Text Society, 1914), 24–25. See too "Gaytryge's Sermon," in *Thornton's MS.*, 12; "The Parson's Prologue and Tale," in Chaucer, *The Canterbury Tales*, sec. 12, ll. 491–92.

13. Ann and Barry Ulanov, *Cinderella and Her Sisters: The Envied and the Envying* (Philadelphia: Westminster Press, 1983).

14. "Of Envy," in Francis Bacon, *The Essayes or Counsels, Civill and Morall* [1625], ed. Michael Kiernan (Cambridge: Harvard University Press, 1985), 28. Bacon notes the possibility of turning one's defects into a source of honor: even lacking as I am, look what I did. . . .

15. Joseph Butler, *Fifteen Sermons* [1749], in *British Moralists 1650–1800*, ed. D. D. Raphael, 2 vols. (Oxford: Clarendon, 1969), 1:344 n.

16. *Rambler*, no. 183.

17. Yury Olesha, *Envy*, trans. T. S. Berczynski (Ann Arbor: Ardis, 1975), 77.

18. See William Aspin, *The Envious Man's Character: A Sermon Preached at Smart's Church in Cambridge* (London, 1684), 16.

19. *Aesop without Morals*, trans. and ed. Lloyd W. Daly (New York: Thomas Yoseloff, 1961), 205.

20. *Rhetoric to Alexander*, 1445ᵃ 19–23. For Aristotle's actual views, contrast *Nicomachean Ethics*, 1108ᵇ 1–5; *Eudemian Ethics* 1221ᵃ 3.

21. Adam Smith, *The Theory of Moral Sentiments* [1790], ed. D. D. Raphael and A. L. Macfie (Oxford: Clarendon, 1976), 244.

22. *Policraticus*, bk. 7, chap. 24, as translated in Joseph B. Pike, *Frivolities of Courtiers and Footprints of Philosophers* (Minneapolis: University of Minnesota Press, 1938),287.

23. John Rawls, *A Theory of Justice* (Cambridge: Belknap Press, Harvard University Press, 1971), 533.

24. "On Transformations of Instinct as Exemplified in Anal Erotism" [1917], in *The Standard Edition of the Complete Psychological Works of Sigmund Freud*, trans. James Strachey and others, 24 vols. (London: Hogarth Press, 1953–1974), 17:129–32; "Analysis Terminable and Interminable" [1937], *Standard Edition*, 23:252.

25. Melanie Klein, *Envy and Gratitude: A Study of Unconscious Sources* (London: Tavistock, 1957). For an entertaining work drawing on psychoanalysis and (just-so stories about) evolutionary biology, see Harold N. Boris, *Envy* (Northvale, N.J.: Jason Aronson, Inc., 1994).

26. Pope to Addison, 20 July 1713, *Letters of Mr. Alexander Pope, and Several of His Friends* (London, 1737), 98.

27. David Hume, *A Treatise of Human Nature* [1739–1740], ed. L. A. Selby-Bigge, 2d ed. rev. P. H. Nidditch (Oxford: Clarendon, 1978), 377. So too Aristotle, *Rhetoric* 1387ᵇ 21–1388ᵃ 19.

28. Bernard Mandeville, *The Fable of the Bees: or, Private Vices, Publick Benefits*, ed. F. B. Kaye, 2 vols. (Oxford: Clarendon, 1924; reprint ed. Indianapolis: LibertyClassics, 1988), 1:136 [1732].

29. Alexis de Tocqueville, *Democracy in America*, intro.

30. "Harrison Bergeron" [1961] in Kurt Vonnegut, *Welcome to the Monkey House* (New York: Delacorte Press, 1968), 7–13.

31. George Bernard Shaw, *The Intelligent Woman's Guide to Socialism and Capitalism* (New York: Brentano's, 1928), 456.

32. Helmut Schoeck, *Envy: A Theory of Social Behaviour* [1966], trans. Michael Glenny and Betty Ross (New York: Harcourt, Brace & World, 1969).

33. Peter I. Rose, "Blaming the Jews," *Society* (September/October 1994) 31(6):39–40; Joshua Muravchik, "Facing Up to Black Anti-Semitism," *Commentary* (December 1995) 100(6):30.

34. Augustine, *City of God*, bk. 14, chap. 28.

35. Sir Philip Sidney, *The Countess of Pembroke's Arcadia* [1590], ed. Maurice Evans (Harmondsworth: Penguin, 1984), 620.

36. Voltaire, *Candide*, chap. 30.

37. Patricia Long, "Want to Create Tomato Envy?" *New Choices for Retirement Living* (March 1993) 33(2):58–60.

# INDEX

# ABOUT THE CONTRIBUTORS

**William H. Gass** is the director of the International Writers Center at Washington University in St. Louis, where he is the David May Distinguished University Professor in the Humanities. He is the author, most recently, of *Cartesian Sonata,* a collection of novellas, and *Reading Rilke.*

**Don Herzog** teaches law and political theory at the University of Michigan. He is the author of *Without Foundations, Happy Slaves,* and *Poisoning the Minds of the Lower Orders.* He is now working on cunning.

**William I. Miller** is the Thomas G. Long Professor of Law at the University of Michigan. His most recent writings—for example, *The Anatomy of Disgust*—have been about the emotions. He is a student of the bloodfeud.

**Jerome Neu** teaches philosophy at the University of California at Santa Cruz. He is the editor of *The Cambridge Companion to Freud* and the author of *Emotion, Thought, and Therapy,* as well as a forthcoming volume: *A Tear Is an Intellectual Thing.*

**James Ogilvy** has pursued two careers, first as a professor of philosophy, second as a consultant. He taught at Yale from 1968 to 1974 and at the University of Texas and Williams College until 1979. He then joined SRI International until 1987, when he and four partners founded Global Business Network. His most recent book is *Living without a Goal.*

**Thomas Pynchon** is the author of *Gravity's Rainbow, Vineland,* and *Mason & Dixon,* among other books.

**Robert C. Solomon** is the Quincy Lee Centennial Professor of Business and Philosophy and Distinguished Teaching Professor at the University of Texas at Austin. He is the author of *From Rationalism to Existenialism, About Love, It's Good Business,* and many other books.

**Elizabeth V. Spelman** is a professor of philosophy at Smith College and the author of *Inessential Woman: Problems of Exclusion in Feminist Thought* and *Fruits of Sorrow: Framing Our Attention to Suffering.* She is tinkering away on a book about the nature of repair.